TAMING THE BULL

September 10, 2004

Mr. John Bramlett
159 Cotton Ridge Cove, South
Cordova, Tennessee 38018

Dear John:

Thank you for the copy of your book, *Taming the Bull*. Your story is an inspiration, and I appreciate the thoughtful inscription. Your kind words mean a lot to me.

Best wishes.

Sincerely,

George W. Bush

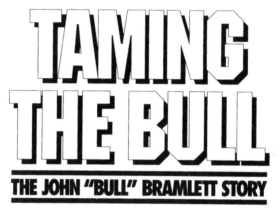

TAMING THE BULL

THE JOHN "BULL" BRAMLETT STORY

John Bramlett with Tula Jeffries

Printed in the United States

Scripture quotations are from THE KING JAMES VERSION of the Bible. Copyright © 1977, Thomas Nelson, Inc., Publishers.

Library of Congress Cataloging-in-Publication Data

Bramlett, John.
    Taming the Bull : the John "Bull" Bramlett story / by John
Bramlett with Tula Jeffries.
        p.   cm.
    Includes bibliographical references.

    1. Bramlett, John.   2. Football players—United States—Biography.
I. Jeffries, Tula, 1921–   II. Title.
GV939.B69A3   1989
796.332'092—dc20
[B]   89-20177
                                                                        CIP

        8 9 10 11 – 02 01 00

To
Warren L. Andrews, Jr.,
my father-in-law, "Pop,"
I dedicate this book.
Proverbs 22:1 is the standard by which he lived:

"A good name is rather to be chosen than great riches, and loving favor rather than silver and gold." He set an example of faithfulness by being faithful to his wife, his children, his church, his business, and his friends. Pop went home to be with Jesus on August 14, 1988, making heaven seem a little nearer to all of us.

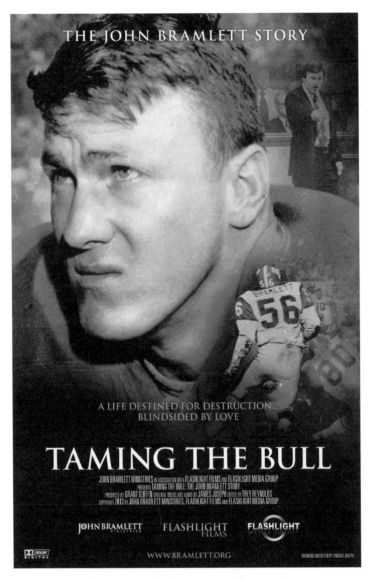

To order a DVD Documentary of
TAMING THE BULL,
The John "Bull" Bramlett story,
go to **www.bramlett.org**

Contents

with
Gratitude

We want to express our heartfelt thanks and deepest appreciation to **Jim Lindsey** and **Gary Cuozzo** for their profound contribution by providing financial assistance in producing this edition of *"Taming the Bull."*

Acknowledgments

I would like to thank many who have tried to help me. Although at the time their efforts may have seemed to fail, I am aware of their impact on the "new man" Jesus Christ has made of me.

My greatest model of unconditional love and understanding is my wife, Nancy, who has been tough enough to honor her marriage commitment through fourteen years of my dishonoring it.

I am grateful to Nancy's parents, Warren and Ad Andrews, for their acceptance of me when my actions were totally unacceptable.

To all the friends who encouraged me to tell my story, I am deeply grateful. Friends who were a part of my early experiences in sports, and those in the professional arena of baseball and football, have all been significant in the development of this book.

I give special thanks to these who took the time to recall in letters and on tape, events from my past: Larry Sutton, Jerry Baskin, Russ Vollmer, Floyd Wooley, Larry Crayton, Jack Counce, Justin Canale, Charlie Haygood, Louis Mullikin, Frank Emanuel, Mike Taliaferro, Stan Mitchell, Barry Brown, Jim Cheyunski, Cliff Polite, Milton Hatcher, Jack Hoelsher, Paul Kuhlman, Clyde Smith, and Chuck Slabaugh.

I also want to thank Eddie and Sue Hanks for their faithful support over the years.

Too numerous to mention are those God brought into my life for His own purposes. They have my heartfelt appreciation as well.

Foreword

Let the reader get ready for an emotional impact. The story you are about to enjoy indeed proves the proverb the truth is stranger than fiction. In this case, it is not only stranger but stronger and more exciting.

John Bramlett is a household name in his hometown of Memphis, Tennessee. A stellar athlete at Memphis State University, he was known to be as fearless as a lion yet "mean as a junkyard dog."

This same reputation followed him into professional sports. John played with such athletic giftedness and reckless abandon that he quickly developed a reputation as the Wild Bull. He was feared, hated, loved, and admired, on and off the playing field.

Then something amazing transpired in this man's life that makes the story you are going to enjoy beautiful and exciting.

It seems, today, that all of the news is bad and the heroes have vanished, the story of John Bramlett will kindle a fire of hope and gratitude in your heart. When John's name is mentioned in Memphis, Tennessee, the citizens almost always react. Some will smile, some will look puzzled, and a few will scowl; but I think I can safely say that almost everyone will speak his name with a sense of respect.

I believe you will be like I was when I read this manuscript: you will find it hard to lay aside until you have finished it. And you will most likely never lose the impact it will have on your life.

Read on and enjoy!

Adrian Rogers, Pastor
Bellevue Baptist Church
Memphis, Tennessee

1

Traveling in Great Company

"Come over and join us, 'Bull,'" a tall man in a gray suit called out. "We need your opinion on something."

"Aw, don't ask him," groaned Marty Schottenheimer, grinning, "or we'll be here all night."

Marty, Dick Butkus, and I were in Boston in 1969 at a convention of truck line executives, drinking their booze while we talked football. As we kidded around, swapping tall stories, I couldn't help thinking, *You can't get it any better than this. Here I am, an invited participant in this big blow-out, being paid $500 to get drunk and have a good time.*

I finished my drink and ambled over to the group at a table. "What was the question?" I asked the tall man who had called me.

"We were talking about the great game you had Sunday," he said, "and we want to know how you got to the play so quickly every time. How do you analyze what you are going to do?"

"Analyze!" I laughed. "Man, you're kidding—who's got time to analyze? You react! If you take the time to think about what you're going to do, it's too late to do it."

"That's right," Marty agreed. "Butkus has been telling you how the man in the middle earns his living. And what Dick Butkus is to middle linebacking is what John Bramlett is to the outside. You've already heard my opinion of him. I say he's the best in the American Conference—no, make that in all of football." Marty, a six-year pro, was a highly-respected Patriots' linebacker himself, but that was Marty, always giving credit to the other players.

Dick Butkus, then a middle linebacker for the Chicago Bears, had just finished explaining to the group how to cut your chances of getting fooled on a play. Butkus had earned his reputation as an unforgettable defensive player; he distracted everybody on opposing teams. It was hard for quarterbacks, tight ends, and running backs to keep their concentration when they knew that a split second after the play began, he was going to be all over whoever had the ball.

Five years of pro football and countless injuries had done nothing to dim my enthusiasm for the game. I never had to work myself up to prepare mentally to play a ball game. I enjoyed the physical contact, I loved the hitting, and as I told Coach Clive Rush at the beginning of my second season with the New England Patriots, I didn't see dollar signs when I played. I told him, "Hey, Coach, I'd play if they didn't pay me. But I have a wife and two boys who like to eat. I don't make unreasonable demands. Just be fair with me, that's all I ask. I love this game."

I knew soon after joining the Patriots that Marty Schottenheimer was more than a great ball player. We spent a part of most Mondays and Tuesdays in the whirlpool together, trying to soak out the aches and pains from Sunday's game. That is when I learned what a great head coach he would be. He could analyze abilities and coordinate moves instantly, going straight to the heart of a problem. I believe that all those talks I had with him helped to make me a better ball player. Today he is a highly respected, winning coach in the National Football League. When I think of all those talks we had, I'm glad so many young players can benefit from his expertise. While he coached the Cleveland Browns, I pulled for him in every game, and now that he is the new head coach of the Kansas City Chiefs, I'll be looking forward to seeing a much improved team there.

For the first twenty-two years of my life, I would never have believed that I could belong with a group like this, enjoying the company of men I admired as much as Schottenheimer and Butkus. I'd been told all my life that I was too small to be competitive in contact sports, but that only made me more aggressive and more determined to prove everyone wrong. In high school and throughout college, I gave everything I had every game, and it was enough. But when the pro scouts told me at graduation that they were not interested in me because of my size, I thought any hope of playing football had ended.

But in January 1965, I signed a contract to play professional football with the Denver Broncos. It was for $12,000. That same year Joe Namath signed with the New York Jets for $400,000. His path to the pros was straight out of the University of Alabama as a high draft pick. My route was not quite as direct. I had played football at Memphis State University, but the pro scouts weren't interested in someone weighing only 173 pounds. In his first season with the Jets, Joe quarterbacked his way into Rookie-of-the-Year. I came in as runner-up for rookie honors, playing outside linebacker with the Broncos.

Players today talk about inequities of salary as if the differences were invented by management in their particular cases. Inequity has always been a factor in sports, just as it is in every other field. The first draft picks can wait for their price to show up on a contract, while the rest scratch and claw just for a chance to sign.

I went to Denver knowing that there was just one way I was going to make the club: by proving that I deserved to be there. I went out every day as if it would be my last chance to prove that I could hit people, and I had known how to do that for most of my 24 years of life. Even before I was 16, I had earned the reputation of being able to outfight any man twice my age! That kind of reputation doesn't just get you into hot water, it keeps the pot boiling. When training camp ended, I wanted to make sure I had a place on the team. I made every practice with the ferocity of a wild bull. (That was not how I came by the nickname "Bull." I got that back in my baseball days when I was playing in the St. Louis Cardinals' farm club in Winnipeg, Canada. But more on that later.) I'll admit that my style of football didn't do anything to suppress my nickname. None of those Bronco ball players had ever heard of me, and there I was out on the field every day, trying to kill them.

On my third day out, Coach Max Speedie was ready to run me

off. "Bramlett," he yelled, "if you want to kill somebody, do it
somewhere else! I'm trying to build a team here. How do you
expect us to win ball games if we don't have any healthy wide
receivers?" He threw in a few unprintable terms to describe my
tackling.

I knew only one way to play, and that was all out. When you
grow up smaller than almost everybody and you still want to play
football, you've got to try to make up the difference someway.

After practice I approached Ray Malavasi, a former member of
the Memphis State University coaching staff. He was responsible
for my being there. "How am I going to prove I can play if I
don't hit people?" I asked. "Do you think they're going to just
take my word for it without my showing them?"

"Don't pay any attention to that stuff," he said. "You get in
there and keep hitting them. The only way you'll get to stay is by
making them remember you."

I shook my head. "I don't know—the coach is pretty upset . . ."

Ray interrupted me. "Don't worry about the coaches. Just
keep on hitting the way you've always done it."

I guess all those fights I got into growing up must have sharp-
ened my instincts. I was fast and I was quick, and believe me,
there is a difference. If you're fast, that means you sometimes can
blitz the quarterback and get to him a split second before he can
get the pass off. Or you can get down field for an interception. Or
get all the way across the field to make a tackle. With quickness,
on the other hand, you develop hair-trigger reflexes. A linebacker
lives by his instincts. An outside linebacker has to worry about
several different blocking combinations, which means you don't
have all day to think about what you need to do. Those fastbacks
coming out of the backfield get by you if you hesitate. I never
forgot what my high school coach, Rube Boyce, once told me.

"Bramlett, what are you supposed to be doing out there?"

"Well, Coach, I thought . . ." Before I could continue, he was
all over me. "*You* thought! What do you mean, *you* thought!
You're not out there to think! I'll do the thinking. You just *do* it!"

So I learned to read the formation, then let my instincts take over. When the ball was snapped, I didn't think about what to do, I just did it, using my body for a battering ram. I could lay a man out with a forearm, or come up under him with a head block that would loosen his teeth. The idea in football is not just to hit, but to leave an impression. Once you get people looking around to see where *you* are, they don't have time to look for the ball.

By the time I arrived in Denver in 1965, I had worked too hard just for a shot at the pros to ever let up. Right after I graduated from high school, scouts from several teams had told me I was too small to play professional football, so I had signed a contract to play baseball with the St. Louis Cardinals. But I was so unmanageable and stirred up so much trouble everywhere I went that I didn't last long in baseball. The day I learned that the Cardinals no longer wanted my services was one of the most devastating days of my life.

Despite my defiance against management, the idea of being out of sports completely was one I had never considered. I was willing to explore any avenue. Eddie Stanky, who had always been good to me as the Cardinals' farm director, had moved to the Mets' club. I called him up. We talked, and he promised to try to help me.

"You're a little rough around the edges," he said, "but that is what we have coaches for. I'll see what I can work out and get back to you."

Considering all the times he had stuck by and defended me when I had messed up with the Cardinals, I was surprised that he still wanted to help me. Eddie Stanky had to have a stubborn kind of faith in humanity that made him hate to give up on a man, because I am sure I tried his patience to the limit. He had gotten me out of jails and had talked authorities into leniency toward me on several occasions. Instead of bawling me out for my misconduct, he attempted in each case to appeal to my sense of obligation to others.

"John," he'd say to me, "you need to stop this drinking and fighting. All it does is get you into trouble. You have a good wife and two fine young sons. You ought to think about what you are doing to them."

When I asked Eddie to help me get back into baseball, I'm sure he believed I was ready to listen. Certainly at that moment I would have promised anything for another chance. But before he had time to talk with the Mets' organization about me, I got a call from Ray Malavasi. Ray had been defensive coordinator for Memphis State University while I played football there.

Ray had gone from Memphis to Wake Forest University as defensive coordinator, where one of his better-known charges was Brian Piccolo. I knew Ray liked the way I played because I heard that he used the Memphis State game films to demonstrate to Wake Forest linebackers how to hit people with velocity. Because he knew I was always looking for someone to hit, he used me as the example. In 1964 he had just recently moved to Denver as player personnel director for the Broncos. When he called, he asked what I was doing, and how big I was. I knew he didn't really want to know what I was doing. His memory of my Memphis State escapades could tell him that, plus the fact that it was no secret that I was still stirring up trouble everywhere I went.

I told him I weighed 182 pounds, which may have been a slight exaggeration. He promised me a tryout with the Broncos if I could tip the scales at 200 by the time training camp opened. Six months can dwindle fast when you are faced with trying to do something that looks impossible. I played my entire four years at Memphis State and gained only ten pounds. But my wife, Nancy, after living with me for five years, had learned to ignore the word "impossible." She had to be a fighter to have survived my vicious temperament up to this point. I don't know if she was trying to prove that I could make it, or that she could, but she took the challenge personally. Putting on twenty pounds didn't seem to her an insurmountable hurdle.

"You are just now getting to the right age to gain weight easily," she argued. "We can do it." When Nancy said "we," she meant it. She hauled out all the rich, fat foods and piled them on. Then she sat at the table with me, watching until the last bite disappeared before she would move a dish. After I stuffed down all I thought I could hold, she would pick up a fork full and hold it in front of me. The first time she did that, I made the mistake of telling her to take it away. Before I got the first word out, she had shoved a big bite of scalloped potatoes into my mouth. "Stop that," I said, and in went another fork full. She used every trick in the book to keep me eating. "Two more bites," she always insisted; "just two little bites." But they were never little.

At bedtime, there she was in front of me with a big malt, not in a glass—that didn't hold enough to suit her. I got it in a big bowl. Then she rolled me off to bed. Along with all of that, I started a weight lifting program, and all of a sudden I was seeing progress.

I arrived at the Denver camp carrying forty-three extra pounds, and I had put them on in six months. Nancy's perseverance had given me my chance; it was up to me to do the rest. Twenty-four years of wanting to be somebody and have something worthwhile gave me all the intensity I needed.

The training camp was at the Colorado School of Mines, at Golden. Some of the rookies grumbled that the high elevation affected their breathing, but to me it was just like breathing anywhere else. After we had been there a week, breathing was not uppermost in our minds anyway; we had a more immediate concern: dysentery. Everybody got it. The team doctors were dispensing drugs and giving shots that dried up everything in the human body except the dysentery. Some of the medicine affected our mouths the same way green persimmons would if you were crazy enough to try to eat them. My mouth got so puckered up that my tongue just curled up when I tried to talk.

"Hol'thit, doc," I mumbled, about the second day. "I know a bether thopper than thith. What we need ith thum Mithithippi Diarrhea Cordial." My mom dosed out that remedy to check the trots when I was just a little kid. All the trainers did was laugh. They thought I was making it up.

We tried making a joke out of it at first. We were not above grabbing some of the smaller guys on their way to the bathroom, and holding them, which always turned out to be a mistake. After a few days nobody was laughing. Middle linebacker Jerry Hopkins and defensive tackle Ray Jacobs had fun pulling practical jokes until dysentery hit them. When they got it, it was almost a relief for the rest of us.

In camp at night, the veterans would make the rookies sing their school fight songs. John Griffin, veteran safety, was also from Memphis State, but he couldn't help me with the songs; he didn't know them any better than I did. When it came my turn, I'd sing the big Elvis Presley hits, "You Ain't Nothin' But a Hound Dog," and "Shake, Rattle and Roll."

Cookie Gilchrist had played Canadian football, then he had come over to the Buffalo Bills where he was AFC Player of the Year, and from there he came on to Denver. Cookie had a fancy new Cadillac with lettering on the side that said, LOOKIE LOOKIE HERE COMES COOKIE. That car had everything on it he could get on it. There was a telephone in it that would blow the horn on every incoming call.

Charlie Parker, offensive guard from the University of Southern Mississippi, was watching Cookie get out of his car one day, and he said, "The way Cookie feels about that car, you know, he'd probably sleep in it if he could stretch out." We were standing at our dorm window of solid plate glass which reached from the bottom floor all the way to the top. From where Charlie and I stood, we could see all three flights of stairs. Cookie's room was on the third floor.

I said, "Charlie, if Cookie's phone started ringing when he was on the top floor, wonder how long it would take him to get to his car?"

Charlie solemnly considered my question. "Well, when he comes in tonight, why don't we find out?"

Cookie was always the last to come in at night, so Charlie and I waited for him. We watched as he climbed the stairs and just as he reached the top floor, we dialed his number. His horn started blowing, and he took off down the stairs about three steps at a time. Just as he got the car door open, we hung up the phone. It was so funny to see him lumbering down those stairs that we kept that going for several nights. Finally, I decided to tell him. Cookie was so big and such an intense kind of guy, I didn't know what he might do. He just laughed and said, "'Bull,' you ain't gonna' make it through the season, you know that? Somebody's bound to take you out!"

He was awesome on the field. He weighed about 250, and was quick as a cat. He played fullback. When he was in the game, the coaches would free some of the tackles to double opposing team players and let Cookie block the tackles' positions. He had a great forearm and was so fast on his feet that it was hard to stay out of his reach.

I remember an exhibition game against the then Oakland Raiders in which a middle screen pass went to Cookie. Our quarterback, Mickey Slaughter, dropped back. Cookie turned, and when he caught the ball, Archie Matsos, Raider middle linebacker, came for him. Archie had timed his move perfectly. He came into Cookie full speed; I mean he threw all of his 220 pounds into that hit, one of the hardest licks I have ever seen. It didn't even phase Cookie. He kept right on going. He ran over Archie like a steam roller, and went on down the field for fifteen or twenty more yards before the Raiders finally got him down.

As I looked back down field, I couldn't believe what I saw. Archie was lying flat on his back with both legs and arms raised straight up in the air, shaking; his whole body was quivering, as though it had taken an electric shock. After a few seconds, his legs and arms slowly lowered to the ground, and a shudder passed through his body. He became still and I figured he was dead. I couldn't see how anyone could have taken that hit and still be alive. Archie was tough. He finally got up, but it was a long while before he could play again. His jaw was broken on both sides.

We received $50 for each exhibition game. I saved my money so I could get an apartment and bring Nancy and the boys to Denver. Andy was five that year, 1965, and Don was four. When we settled into an upstairs furnished apartment, the first thing Nancy wanted to know was, "Who lives here that we know? Who are our friends?" She was hoping I had met some nice football players with nice wives. She already knew not to expect to find Andy and Don many playmates among my teammates. We married younger than most of them. Not many of the ones I knew had given much thought to long-term commitments. Neither had I, but Nancy thought enough about that for both of us.

We fought a lot over how married people were supposed to live.

"You've got to grow up sometime," she would say. I hated that.

"What do you mean, grow up?" I would yell, not in just those words. To me, growing up meant being able to do more of what I had always done: cussing, chewing, drinking, fighting, and a lot of other stuff she seemed to find objectionable. I stayed out all night many times because I knew Nancy was going to be looking at me with those big blue eyes, wondering where I had been, and lying to her was going to make me feel like a dog. Then I'd get angry, throw stuff around, and break a few things.

Before we played our first regular season game, I already had earned the reputation of being a mean so-and-so. My teammates respected me for the hard-nosed way I had earned my position, but this same attitude carried over into everything I did. I thought I had to outdo everybody. Those guys were probably amazed that someone could keep up the pace I did—or would even want to. In only a few weeks, they were all calling me "Bull," but I was so wild and unpredictable that most of them were careful about where they went with me. I was likely to get them involved in a brawl or get us all thrown in jail.

On the football field I was vicious, I was reckless, and I was out there with one purpose: to stop people. Linebackers make contact with enthusiasm or it doesn't count, but the aggression needs to be left on the field. My problem was a deeply-rooted hostility that governed everything I did on or off the field. My willingness to fight was well documented.

By the time I made the Bronco team, the pro football arena was so important to me that I was never able to see it as only a part of the real world. To me, it was the whole thing, the only reality. During the six months that I was working my guts out in Memphis just to get to try out for the team, I didn't drink, smoke, or chew. I didn't even have time to fight. I was so busy running sprints, lifting weights, doing programmed exercising, and eating that nothing else mattered. Running up a hill out by the light, gas, and water subdivision became routine after awhile, so I started running up it backwards. That is tough, but it builds legs that won't quit on you after three quarters of football in which the defense has to spend too much time on the field. Six months of total abstinence from my usual vices must have made it even harder than I ever realized for Nancy to adjust to life in Denver. But as soon as I made the team, I went right back to my old ways, trying as hard as I could to make up for all the carousing I had missed. The Denver police soon knew me by name. They often arrested me for disorderly conduct without even booking me. They knew Ray Malavasi had taken me under his wing, and out of respect for him they eased up on me.

That first year in Denver was exciting to me. I can see now that to Nancy, it was just a big disappointment. Away from her family and friends, she had the full responsibility of the boys. I am sure she hoped that once I realized my life-long dream of doing something on my own, of being recognized as a professional athlete, I would let up on the wild life at least a little. But I was so caught up in what I was doing, I couldn't see anything else. Football, drinking, and partying made up the only world I wanted. I was thrilled to be associating with well-known personalities, and I felt good about the publicity I was getting. Here I was, just a free agent, and suddenly I was being talked about as a contender for Rookie-of-the-Year.

I was fortunate to have men like Ray Malavasi and George Dickson pulling for me from my first day in Denver. I worked hard, but a lot of others did too, with several players vying for the same position. I credit the counsel I got from Malavasi and Coach Dickson, who worked with the defensive backs, in giving me the edge. The Denver newspapers carried quotes from Coach Dickson to the effect that "Bramlett never gives you 100 per cent . . . it is always 200 per cent." He said, "There never has been a better hard-nosed football player to come on as fast as Bramlett in his first pro season." As cynical as I was about everything, I really was humbly grateful to those two great men.

The Commercial Appeal of Memphis repeated a quote from Coach Max Speedie that appeared in the Denver papers: "We definitely think Bramlett has a shot at rookie-of-the-year honors in the American Football League. After only two months of play, I think he deserves to be No. 1, and he is improving every game."

Coach Speedie mentioned others in the running: Joe Namath,

tackle Gerry Philbin of New York, halfback Gene Foster of San Diego, and fullback Jim Nance of Boston.

Nothing could have surprised me more than Coach Speedie's support. Only a short time before, he had threatened to run me off, insisting that I was going to kill all of his wide receivers. I could hardly believe it when he called a team meeting and told the players: "If we seem to be giving Bramlett more publicity than you fellows think is his share, it is because the recognition is necessary to help his chances for 'top rookie' honors. You all agree that he deserves it."

I liked the hubbub of the pro football world, but even while I was right in the middle of it, I noticed something strange. I was doing things I never believed could happen, and yet, unexplainably, they didn't satisfy me. It was an honor to be asked on as a guest to the TONIGHT SHOW while Johnny Carson talked about me as a candidate for Rookie-of-the-Year—but it was not the thrill I expected.

I stayed so tense, so on edge, and so unsatisfied with everything that came my way that years later one of my former baseball buddies commented that before he met me, he had never known anyone who was mad twenty-four hours a day, every day.

In several games during 1965, I played with injuries that should have kept me off the field. I told myself it was worth it when I was the only rookie to make any of the All-Pro teams that year.

But I was not chosen as Rookie-of-the-Year. As it turned out, Joe Namath was as great a quarterback as the New York Jets had hoped he would be, and he received the award. I agreed with their choice; he deserved it. Hey, I still felt like I was traveling in great company.

2

573 Alabama Street

I grew up in Memphis, Tennessee, in a rambling old house on the north side of town. It was a poor neighborhood, but none of us thought of it that way, because we were all poor. Something about sharing a situation with others keeps you from feeling like it's the end of the world, even if it is bad. We always had food on the table and clothes to wear, and there was always something fun to do when we weren't working. I remember the clothes we all wore had patches, and our shoe soles had holes in them. But as I said, "What are you going to do, walk up to someone with holes in his shoes and say, 'Hey, look, I've got a bigger hole in my shoe than you'?" It was pretty much the same for all of us who lived on Alabama Street. Nobody made more of our situation than it actually was.

Our house had extremely high ceilings, making it difficult to heat. It was always drafty in the winter. Hitting the floor with bare feet on a cold morning no doubt accounts for my total recall of walking down the long hall through the house and outside across the back porch to reach the bathroom. It was one place you went only in response to nature's urgent call, never just to enjoy a few moments of privacy or to dawdle over the morning paper.

As gripping as the cold was in winter, the summer heat made us melt. A big fan installed in a window made the living room fairly comfortable, but I remember the fan because of what happened one Sunday more than for its cooling power. My mom and dad, my brother Bobby, and I were sitting in the living room talking, when all of a sudden our cat, "Baby," came flying through the window, right between the blades of the window fan. We never

figured out how "Baby" timed her leap so as to come through
without a scratch. Years later, when I was working out to gain
more quickness in sports, just when I would think I had reached
my limit, I would remember "Baby" coming through that window with the fan running full speed, and I'd go back to work.

There was a housing development, Lauderdale Courts, on our
street, and close by it was a big, open field that we called The
Triangle. All the neighborhood kids met there to play touch football, baseball, corkball, or just to goof off. A lack of equipment
never bothered us. We all liked to play corkball. Someone would
cut the broomstick off of a worn out broom for the "bat." The
ball, or "corkball," was made by carefully taping a thermos bottle
cork. A good one required the kind of tape hospitals use, one-
fourth inch width white adhesive; it was the only kind that was
pliable enough. It took skill to wrap a corkball right. We played
that game right on the streets. Games sometimes lasted from
eight in the morning until eight at night as kids came and went.
Before I was nine years old, I was playing corkball, and going
down to The Triangle with my older brothers, usually sticking
with Charles Clayton, who was six years my senior.

There were five boys in the Bramlett family. J.M., Odell, and
Charles were all older than me, then came Bobby, who was
the youngest. Odell and Charles had a friend who lived across the
street from the courts, Elvis Presley. I liked Elvis because he
never seemed to mind having me around. He did call me "little"
Bramlett, but I figured he used the term for identification rather
than to put me down. Later on we became friends. After we went
our separate ways, we occasionally got together with others from
the old neighborhood. Elvis liked to play touch football. I don't
think he ever outgrew it; after I married, whenever he got back to
Memphis, he wanted us to get a group together to play touch
football. Elvis went to Humes High, but he was already out by
the time I got there.

My brothers and I all had jobs when we were not in school. The
older boys had paper routes or worked part-time delivering groceries. Odell liked to bellhop in the hotels; tips were good and the
old Claridge Hotel had something interesting going on all the

time. I followed Odell so much of the time, I was referred to by his friends as "The Shadow." It was a sad day for me when he joined the Marines, but I was proud of him. He became a sea-going Marine right out of boot camp, an unusual feat, but he was a hard worker.

Before I was old enough to have my own newspaper route, I tagged along behind Charles, helping with his.

"Charles Clayton," I'd ask every day, "do you think we can get a hot doughnut? They're just a nickel."

"Yeah. I guess."

Thinking about the bakery over on Poplar Street could shorten the two-mile walk by half. They made big oatmeal-raisin cookies that you could smell baking from a block away.

"What about a cookie, Charles Clayton?" I'd ask.

"What about a cookie?" he would tease.

I idolized my brothers and wanted to be just like them. If one of them had a date, I went along and waited outside on the curb till he got ready to go home. Running around with older boys might not have been what made me aggressive, but it probably helped to bring it on earlier. Everybody seemed to be bigger than I was; I thought it was up to me to prove I was tougher. I took on anybody—anytime—anyplace! With an attitude like that, I was in a fight just about every day.

Hostility won't make you tough, but if you are going to get hostile with bigger guys, you had better be tough. My junior high football coach used to say that a mean little guy who would hang in there made a lot better defensive player than one twice his size who didn't like to hit. His theory was that the little guy had to be tough to survive what his hostilities got him into, while the big boy was trying to learn something that wasn't a part of his nature because he didn't feel that he had to prove anything. I was small enough to furnish living proof to the coach's theory, but my hostility was never limited to the playing field.

Before I got out of junior high at Humes, I was already a familiar figure to the area's hospital repair units. When I was three, I fell on a sharp stick that split my throat open. By the time I was seven, I had moved on to more purposeful action, involving others. Once during a rock fight, a rock split my face open from the nostrils down through my upper lip.

I had a bad habit of running with my tongue sticking out of my mouth, my teeth clamped down on my tongue. It became a family joke that I had to get my mouth fixed right before I could run. But one play in an overhead tackle game ended the joke and broke that habit for good. In a game at Winchester Park in Memphis, I was running in my usual manner when I made a tackle. As I dived for the ball carrier, his heel came up and caught me under the chin. My teeth cut all the way through my tongue, leaving it barely hanging by a little piece of skin. I don't remember many injuries hurting as much as that one. When I was able to get on my feet, one of the boys loaded me on his bicycle and pedaled me to the doctor's office with my tongue hanging out of my mouth like a strip of raw meat.

By the time the doctor stitched me back together, my tongue had started swelling. It was days before I could get it all back in my mouth, and weeks before the soreness subsided. I entered junior high and began football practice in the fall with my mouth still so sensitive that it hurt to eat.

Humes High housed grades seven through twelve. Humes Junior High included the seventh through ninth grades. It was there that I spent the best and the worst of times. The best came after three o'clock with the hitting and tackling of football practice. The worst, not surprisingly, was struggling to conjugate a verb, or trying to figure out how to get a book report in by a deadline when I had no intention of reading the book—any book.

It was the good fortune of every boy who loved football to have Coach Lee Thompson as his mentor. He taught the fundamentals of football. He taught the principles by which the game should be played. He taught the rudiments of proper attitude. And he taught them by example.

I must have learned more from Coach Thompson than I realized at the time. The broader implications of attitude escaped me to a degree, but I think that was because I was so absorbed in the basics of the game: how to hold the ball, carry the ball, throw the ball; how to roll out, how to hit, how to throw a forearm, how to throw a block. The backs were taught how to take a handoff. I learned how to line down in a three-point stance, how to fire out, and how to make a crossbody block. One of the coach's main goals was to teach us to be innovative in every situation. Lacking the sophisticated equipment afforded the varsity team, he improvised. For tackling dummies, he used a blown-up inner tube pulled together in the middle and held with a wide rubber band. A player could then hook his hand in the band and hold the inner tube in front of his body while the other players practiced hitting it. This was just one of the ways he kept us abreast of workout routines in every phase of football. Coach Thompson was the definitive coach. He believed that every player needed to understand the mechanics of every position on the team.

In the spring he just as precisely taught the basics of baseball, showing us how to lay down a bunt and how to slide properly.

When I came out for football in junior high, none of the seventh graders knew how to use the gear and suit out. We tried to avoid the upperclassmen until we could figure out how to get the uniforms on. Most of us had never seen a jock strap. The three-piece hip pads had us totally baffled. Coach Thompson tried to hide his smile when he saw what we did with them. When we finally got them on, we had the protective tailbone piece turned to the frontal area of our bodies, covering the lower part of our anatomies.

Seventh, eighth, and ninth graders all practiced together, which meant that the youngest and often the smallest lined up against the heavyweights. This also carried over to the regular season games with opposing schools.

Some people are considered injury prone, but that doesn't really explain anything. Some get injured through carelessness, others because they are too small for what they are doing. I was constantly getting hurt. I weighed 98 pounds that first year. In scrimmage I tackled Don Armstrong, who weighed 150 pounds, and broke my left ankle. In the eighth grade I broke my other ankle. I managed to squeak through ninth grade football without injury, but going into spring football practice, I broke my left hand. Baseball began while my wrist was still in a cast, but I played anyway.

Being small could have accounted for some of my injuries, but that is not the whole picture. My stubbornness and my utter disregard for common sense put me in jeopardy in any competition. The craving to be on top was always there, driving me. I wanted to be as good as my brother Charles, who had earned an athletic scholarship to Arkansas State College in Jonesboro, Arkansas. When he left home, I was more determined than ever to make him proud of me.

Through weeks of scrimmaging, I went all out, suffering the agony of wondering if I would get a chance to play in a game while Charles was home for a visit. My dream died the Friday afternoon that I hit Don Armstrong and broke an ankle.

My continuing lack of caution brought more grief the following year. Still weighing little more than a hundred pounds, I was just beginning to see game action when I broke the other ankle. After I spent a week in the hospital, Coach Thompson counseled my mother, "Mrs. Bramlett, John is too little for football. I don't think you should let him play."

My mother shook her head. "I know you're right. But I don't know how to stop him. He wants to so bad."

The coach just laughed and walked away. He understood her problem all too well. I don't think it surprised anyone when my cast came off prior to the doctor's projected date for removal. Knowing I would not be allowed to play otherwise, I took a hammer and a saw and cut the cast off. Fortunately, the ankle had healed fast. Casts never lasted long on me.

I began my freshman year weighing 135 pounds, ready for anything. I was dipping Garrett Sweet Snuff, smoking cigarettes, and beginning to see that girls were more fun than I had originally thought. I was still small for football, but I was more determined than ever. Most of my teammates—Jerry Baskin, Larry Young, Leon Weldon, Larry Cox, Bobby Moore, Jimmy Godwin, Bobby Biggs, Jim Alexander, Bobby Wiginton—had made noticeable gains during the summer. They were my friends, but I always felt like I had to prove myself to everybody. It did not occur to me that others had little or nothing to do with my hunger to excel. I recognized limitations in myself; I just didn't accept them. Because I wouldn't accept them, I was out to make sure that no one else did. I am sure Coach Thompson could see the chip on my shoulder, but he chose to ignore it.

The season's schedule had Humes Junior High pretty evenly matched with other schools, except in one instance. South Side, an arch rival, had established itself as the nemesis of all the other area teams because of their quarterback. Chuck Tempfer weighed 210 pounds and was over six feet tall. South Side seldom bothered with more than one play on offense: a roll out right or a roll out left. When the ball was snapped, opposing teams always came with too little, too late.

The week before the big game, big because it was the game that had to be played before any kind of winning mentality could be established, the coach came up with a daring approach. Getting ready to scrimmage, we looked up in amazement at Coach Thompson bearing down on us in full football uniform.

Fastening his helmet, he said, "All right, men, let's find out if you can play this game! I want to see an offensive line in front of me, and the rest of you are going to learn how to hit a big man."

We looked up and down his six-foot-two, 210-pound frame, wondering if this was some kind of joke. It wasn't. Before the week was out, we had learned how to throw all our weight into the coach and roll so as to reduce the impact of the hit to our own bodies.

At first we tackled reluctantly, unsure if the coach's patience was equal to his determination, but as we got into the spirit of it, we were tackling relentlessly. Later, lying awake in my bed the night before the big game, I was thinking, not about Chuck Tempfer, but about what Coach Thompson had done. What would make a man do that? I had seen him get up slowly after being gang tackled; I had watched him touch his rib cage under his jersey. I could still hear the intensity in his voice in that last practice: "Come after me, men! Hit me now! Really hit me!" And all of a sudden I thought I had the answer to what had been puzzling me. Coach Thompson did what he did because he believed in us—he believed we could win! And he was willing to make the sacrifice necessary to give us our chance.

This same realization seemed to have infected the whole team. The afternoon of the game, we got dressed quickly and quietly. The coach walked among us in the locker room, patting our shoulders, giving a word of advice here and there with a big smile on his face.

"Men," he said, "you have done a good job. You have worked hard. Now we are going out there to show them what you're made of. Are you ready for this game?"

A prolonged yell drowned his voice.

Peering out from under his eyebrows at us, he asked, "Can you handle Tempfer?"

More yells, this time louder. Coach Thompson's boys were ready.

"Let's go get 'em," he said quietly, and we trotted out onto the field.

It rained all the next day, but no one could have convinced Coach Lee Thompson or the rest of us that we were not walking in sunlight. In front of both schools, we had beaten South Side. We had knocked the big quarterback, Tempfer, out of the game in the second quarter. The details quickly faded in importance, leaving with us the sweet taste of self-confidence and the greater discovery that having your back against the wall is not the time to quit.

We knew Coach Thompson cared about us, but we also knew better than to translate those feelings into any hope of inconsistency. He was a stickler for good grades. Well versed in our weaknesses, he still insisted on passing grades. On report card days, he lined us up in the locker room, cards in our hands. As he worked his way down the line, a mental count was going on in our minds: an F for academics meant three licks from the thick paddle hanging by the water fountain; an F on conduct got you six.

The coach conscientiously carried out his ruling, with some enthusiasm, I might say. Only once did I see him slack off a little, and that must have been because he was laughing on the inside too hard to get a firm grip on the paddle. We were all standing stiffly in line, waiting our turn. Clyde Nolan, a left-handed quarterback given more to athletics than academics, was next. The coach carefully examined the card, then looked searchingly at Clyde.

"Clyde . . . is this right?"

"No, sir. I don't think so."

"What do you mean, it's not right? It says here, you have two F's in your subjects, and one F in conduct."

"Yes, sir—I mean no, sir."

"What is it, Clyde?"

"Well, I got 'em, but I know it's not right for me to get 'em."

"Clyde, can you count?" The coach reached for the paddle.

"Yes, sir."

"Well, how many licks am I going to give you?"

"Coach, I b'lieve that's twelve." Clyde turned and bent over, his hands on his knees.

When the first lick from the paddle met Clyde's rear, it sounded like it bounced off cotton, without the usual resounding splat-t-t.

Coach Thompson's mouth worked, his eyes narrowed. He said, "Clyde, that didn't sound right."

"Oh, yeah, Coach, it did. It's all right."

"Clyde . . . drop your pants," the coach ordered.

Worse than our own anticipated paddling was our not being able to laugh at Clyde's attempt to soften his punishment. He had put on baseball sliding pads under his clothes.

Coach Thompson was a great man who never backed away from responsibility. Knowing that lectures would soon be forgotten without an example to follow, he taught us by the way he lived. Even the best examples never seemed to have much effect on me. I wanted to be treated in a way that made me feel good, but I felt no sense of responsibility for how others felt. If I did something for another person, it was because it pleased me. I constantly reminded myself, *If you let your guard down with peo-*

ple, they're going to get you. So instead of applying the principles I saw in people such as Coach Thompson, I covered myself with a mean image and acted like I had jumped into wet cement with it.

I looked up to Coach Thompson, but there was no way to survive with such an attitude at 573 Alabama. At least, that's what I believed.

3

Whiskey, Elvis, and Snake

Times were hard, living conditions were often miserable, and I resented it. One day I was playing barefoot in patched britches and having a great time. Suddenly I was looking at the holes in my shoes and clothes, and my circumstances weren't funny any more. Somehow I had realized that to everyone else, poor people were in some way inferior. I couldn't come to terms with that, so I reacted with the only force I recognized: anger. To show authority was to wave a red flag in my face!

I thought I was considered tough to cuss and use bad language in tense situations. Not that I cleaned up my language in easier times; I just tried to match the language to the pressure. I was growing up, anxious to leave behind the restrictions of authority, and ready to try all the "big time" stuff.

Everything I ever learned, I learned the hard way, and drinking was no exception. From the standpoint of enjoyment, I still wonder why anybody would go through what I did to learn to like alcohol. A friend got some "white lightnin'" and got several boys together to try it. Out behind the fence, we passed it around. I wanted to look as if I knew what I was doing, so I turned up the bottle and chug-a-lugged its contents. I killed it, and there for awhile I thought it was going to return the favor.

My insides were on fire. I was blinking and trying to catch my breath when I heard old Jerry Baskin say, "Man, that is *good!* Ain't that *good,* John?"

I managed to choke out, "What'chu talkin' about? 'Man, that is *good!*'" It was awful! After everyone left, I went behind a tree and got sick. I don't mean I felt nauseous, I mean a down-on-the-ground, heaving-up, just-let-me-die kind of sick. After I could sit up I thought, *There has to be a better way to do this.* I wanted to do it, but I preferred not to die doing it. *I'll learn,* I told myself. *I will just go at it gradually.*

I learned that beer and whiskey were smoother going down and calmer when they got there than the bootleg stuff, so I began swiping my brother's ID cards to get into beer joints to buy beer and whiskey.

"Hey, Jerry, you wanta' go downtown? I've got the ID's."

"Got me one too?"

"I wouldn't be askin' you if I didn't."

Jerry and I had a system for just about everything. We figured out ways to cheat kids out of their money by working together, then we'd flip coins with anybody who wasn't on to us. This usually kept us in enough cash to buy a bottle for the week. When we came up short, we sold programs for the football games. The person selling the most programs received a dollar. It didn't take long for Jerry and me to find that together we could outsell anyone. We'd combine our sales and let one or the other collect the prize. We were both going to drink the booze anyway.

When Jerry's mother went to work, we would hotfoot it over to his house and brew a big pot of coffee. Then we would pour the booze in and drink the whole thing. This got to be a ritual on the days we played a game. Sometimes we were out there playing when our breath would have blown the top off the Richter scale. My gradual indoctrination into pleasurable drinking was a success; I could hold more of it than in the beginning, and I could enjoy the buzz without getting sick—that is, unless I got really tanked.

With all my other interests—football, paper routes, odd jobs, drinking, fighting—it is not surprising that I was not your everyday model student. In fact, I was not a model student any day. I didn't find the curriculum very interesting, and my grades reflected it. I cheated my way through school without once thinking that I was the one being cheated. I could always find someone who would allow me to copy what I needed, at least enough to get me a passing grade. That, and the fact that teachers most likely passed me to be rid of me, got me to my junior year at Humes High.

A story went around that once during a test, I was copying from a boy whose desk was next to mine. In answer to one question, he wrote, "I can't explain this," and the story went that I answered the same question with "I can't explain it either."

At Christmas in my junior year, my grandparents came from Huron, Tennessee, to visit us. I liked having them there; the added confusion of having the house full meant a better chance for me to slip out to go drinking with my brothers. There was always plenty of booze at Christmas, but because my mother hated the drinking, we sneaked around to do it.

When my grandparents were ready to go home, J.M. and I took them to Huron in J.M.'s station wagon. By the time we got to their place, all the booze was gone and we were wanting more. My granddad, "Paw," said, "If one of you boys can drive, I know where there's some good 'white lightnin.' But I ain't ridin' with no drunk."

"I can drive, 'Paw,'" I said. "I'm in good shape."

"All right," he agreed, "if you say so. Get in boys—let's go."

The "boys" were my Uncle Johnny and J.M. I was not as drunk as the others, but definitely not in as "good shape" as I claimed. Barreling down a little two-lane country road, I drove, carefully straddling the middle without a thought that anything larger than a squirrel could be coming from the other direction.

J.M. and Uncle Johnny were whooping and hollering like crazy, but "Paw" was serious. "You looka here, John Cameron," he said to me. "I don't care which side of this road you drive on, but you oughta' make up your mind about it. You're hoggin' the whole road."

I pulled over a little and stepped on the gas. I topped a rise in the road going about 65 or 70 MPH and a wheel went off the edge of the road and blew out. I lost control, and the station wagon flipped over. It bounced around and came to a stop on the other side of the road, pointing toward the opposite way. We were half in, half out of the ditch, leaning far over on the side. Nobody was hurt. We were all still sitting upright. Finally, I climbed out and went looking around to see if anyone lived nearby. I found a farmer who had a tractor. He gathered up some chains and came down to pull us out. All of the time he was working to get our car out of the ditch, that old fellow kept shaking his head as if he couldn't believe we had lived through it.

As I think back to that incident, I am amazed at our reaction. After all of that, it never once occurred to me and apparently not to the others that we were alive and unhurt only because of God's providential care—that he might possibly have a reason for keeping us alive.

When we found that the station wagon would still run, there was some discussion about our distance away from the 'white lightnin.' "Paw" made the decision. "I'm for going home," he said. "If we end up having to walk, it's going to be a lot further back than it was comin' out." After we got back to Huron, J.M. and I pried the metal away from the wheels so they wouldn't drag and started to Memphis. The way the engine was missing, we weren't sure it would hold up for the one-hundred-mile trip.

We spent seven hours on the road before we finally limped into Memphis. We had driven at a pace of 15 MPH all the way!

Our family never showed any affection, so I am sure my brothers never knew how much I looked up to them. I wanted to be like them. When we fought, I saw it as a temporary personality clash, over as quickly as it started. On the drive home from Huron, I decided to give J.M. the money to have his station wagon repaired. I had worked ever since I got big enough to throw papers.

When J.M. got the bill for having his car fixed, I offered to pay for it. "You're gonna' pay for it?" he asked. "What are you planning to use for money, Mr. Rockefeller?"

"I've got it," I told him. "Just tell Mama to get it for you." He didn't know I had $500 in the bank. For years I had been giving everything I made to my mother, and she had saved it. We got the car out of the shop and I payed for it—probably one of the few times that I impressed my oldest brother.

❏   ❏   ❏

When Elvis Presley suddenly burst on the public stage to a standing ovation, it shocked all of us who knew him best. As far as I could see, he made no effort to be recognized beyond his own circles. The Suzore Theater on Main Street was a favorite Friday night hangout as I grew up. Before I was old enough to go alone, Odell, Charles, and Elvis took me along when they went to catch the current episode of their serial. Every Friday night the theater showed a chapter, always ending with a crisis so you had to come back the next week to see what happened. Going to the Suzore, we always took along two sticks—one to hold up our seats, the other to beat off the rats. Elvis, my brothers, and I were there one night when Gladys Presley came down to the Suzore looking for Elvis. When she finally saw him, she excitedly began explaining to him that Dewey Phillips had played on the air a tape Elvis had made of "That's All Right" and was asking for Elvis to come to the radio station. I knew he had been playing his guitar and singing on Alabama Street outside the Scotland Inn, a little beer joint. Crowds would gather to hear him, but nobody was very impressed.

Elvis seemed to find it a little hard to believe. He kept asking his mother, "Are you serious?" She said, "Come on; I'll bet they have had a hundred phone calls." When Dewey played the song, people began calling in to ask who the singer was. After dozens of calls, the radio station manager wanted Elvis to come and be interviewed on the air. George Klein, a disc jockey at Station WHBQ, knew Elvis from Humes High and was more than willing to promote Elvis's songs. "That's All Right" was his first big hit, and others soon followed. That first time people heard him and became excited by his voice was probably the last time anyone ever called a radio station to ask who he was. Even at the beginning of his career, Elvis had a voice that, once heard, was not easily forgotten.

I was happy for a friend from the neighborhood to get to do what he loved and enjoy some success with it. At the time, I was feeling pretty good about myself. I had gotten my weight up to 160 and was playing good football. I had picked up on some facets of the game that made the difference between being a really

good player and just making the team. I had gained speed; I had
learned how to read a play and get to the ball. I knew how to use
my headgear like a weapon. I could come up with a head butt and
jolt a man off the ground. I was playing left guard and left linebacker.

I got along better with my coaches than with any others in positions of authority, possibly because I didn't want to jeopardize
my chance to play football. In other places, I was constantly getting into trouble. My attitude in the classroom, bad at the beginning, went steadily downhill.

We had ROTC in high school, and I took an immediate dislike
to everything connected with it. I hated the uniforms, I didn't
like it when the ROTC officers called me "Mr. Bramlett" in their
sneering, superior way, and I had not learned to tolerate anyone
giving me orders. One day out on the grounds, a lieutenant said
something I didn't understand. I turned and said, "I didn't hear
you." He answered with what I considered a smart remark and
without thinking, I hit him in the face with my fist. Before I
could be stopped, I knocked him down and messed up his face.
Those in authority could never seem to figure out a form of discipline that would work with me. That time, they called my dad,
then suspended me for several days. Punishment angered me; it
never impressed me with a need to change. Sergeant Hatley, who
headed the ROTC unit, was a kind man who actually went out of
his way to try to help me, but I was so rebellious I would not
respond in a reasonable way to anyone.

My reputation for fighting and starting trouble kept things
stirred up everywhere I went. I hung out around places where
trouble was likely. Sailors and marines came into town from the
naval base at Millington in suburban Memphis, and they were
quick to respond to a challenge, especially after a few drinks.
When my buddies and I were drinking, we were naturally antagonistic. In no time at all we could get a full-scale battle going with
those sailors and marines. This was not one of those scrapes
where a truce could be called if it got rough. People sometimes
got badly hurt—teeth knocked out, bones broken, bruises and
cuts that had to be stitched up.

Every neighborhood had its own tough group. Lauderdale Courts, Lamar Terrace, and Winchester Park each had a bunch of tough guys. Hurt Village held the distinction of being the worst of all. Their leader was known as "Snake." He was overbearing and intimidating. I don't know who gave him the name, but it was said that if you had a tolerance of snakes, being around him would make you rethink your position. Even with my uncontrollable temper, I didn't think of myself as being a bad person; most of my outbursts were circumstantial as far as I was concerned. I justified my explosiveness by convincing myself that if someone took it upon himself to cross me, it constituted excessive and undue provocation. So I guess it was inevitable that I would have to tangle with Snake.

I was hustling popcorn, cotton candy, and Cokes at the auditorium. It was circus week, which was one of the more profitable events. You can sell an incredible amount of food and drink to little kids caught up in all the hullabaloo of animals, clowns, and acrobats.

The management provided jackets with insignia for the working personnel. I had my own jacket, with pockets for carrying my change, and I was proud of it. The first day of the circus I checked in early, then decided to wait for more people to arrive before starting to work. I went out to look around for awhile, but before leaving I gave my jacket to Vernon Elrod, a teammate from Humes High, and asked him to keep it for me. When the stands began to fill, I went back to pick up my jacket.

Vernon said, "Uh, John . . . your jacket isn't here."

"Where is it?"

"Snake came by," he said. "He took it."

That disturbed me a little. My next question was meant to disturb him. "What do you mean, 'He took it'? Didn't you tell him it was mine?"

"Yeah, I told him. He said he didn't care whose it was. He was going to wear it."

So Snake was selling cold drinks, wearing my jacket, and I was left standing there. I knew he would be back, so I decided to wait there for him. The longer I waited, the more I convinced myself that Snake was not going to keep my jacket; it was mine, and I was going to get it back.

When he came in, I said, "Snake, that's my jacket you are wearing."

He looked at me. "You know, I don't see your name on it," he said.

I stood there looking back at him. "Snake, I want my jacket back."

He said, "The only way you are going to get *this* jacket is to take it."

I had already taken his size into account. He was quite a lot bigger than I was. What I had not taken into account was the switchblade knife in his hand. When he told me I would have to take the jacket by force, he popped open the switchblade.

I thought it over and made a decision. "If that's the way you're going to be," I said, "you just keep the jacket."

I turned around with my back to him and heard the click of the knife as he closed it. As it snapped shut, I wheeled back toward him and hit him squarely in the mouth with my fist. I dropped him right there. As he hit the concrete floor, I kicked him and went for the knife. If I had gotten my hands on the knife, I am not sure what I would have done to Snake. In all probability I would have killed him with it, but by then people were all around us trying to drag me off of him. Before they stopped me, I had busted his lip and caused one of his eyes to swell shut.

The cops came and arrested Snake for pulling the knife on me. I was called to court the next morning to testify against him. The incident didn't do anything to improve my image. It was the kind of story that people like to add details to. When it got around, it just stirred up more aggressive action for me.

4

Walkin' "Chollie"

George P. Everitt is a name that to me is almost synonymous with baseball. He must have been in his early seventies when I first met him. He was the manager and coach of the Coca Cola Travelers, a semi-pro team that played throughout the mid-South. An avid supporter of school sports, he chose his recruits by watching the newspaper stories about the best players on the high school and college teams.

Mr. Everitt drove a panel truck. He was a pie salesman, but that was secondary; he would unload those pie racks at the drop of a pin and start loading benches in the back of the pie truck. That was how the team traveled to the places they played, places such as Helena, Arkansas; Holly Springs, Mississippi; and Ripley, Tennessee. I enjoyed playing for Mr. Everitt, but I didn't ride a bench in his team bus much after the first few times. He always smoked a cigar. He would light up, get started talking, and pretty soon he would be driving down the left side of the street, still spinning his yarn. His preference for the wrong side of the street raised some doubts in my mind as to safety, so I usually managed to find other transportation.

Among all those legendary characters who impress you with both their strategy and their lack of it, Mr. Everitt was a standout. He had worked out an artful set of signals for his players to use during a game. If he touched his hat, he wanted you to hit; if he touched his belt, he wanted a bunt. When he brushed his hand across his shirt, he expected you to steal a base. His signs for a squeeze play were a little more complicated. He sat on a little folding chair during the game, and when he got up, folded up his chair, unfolded it, then sat back down in it, he meant for you to get ready to make a squeeze play. His signals were no trouble to read; the trouble was that the teams we played knew them as well as we did! We probably couldn't have handled a more complex system, but the simplicity of it made it easy for opposing teams to anticipate our plays. The signals were not all that significant anyway, considering that boys jumped from team to team and passed all their inside information around.

Some of the boys had nicknamed Mr. Everitt "Walkin' Chollie." I never knew why they called him that, but it didn't really matter because it was a term of affection. He loved all the boys and was involved in their lives. He was a thin man of average height, but strong and full of energy. His blue eyes would snap with excitement when the subject of baseball came up, which was any time you talked to him. It is not entirely accurate to say you talked to him; somehow you always ended up listening while Mr. Everitt talked. He liked to tell stories of other times and places, and he always remembered some that he felt would bear repeating. I heard most of them several times.

I am sure he noticed after awhile that I always borrowed a glove when I played, so one day he called me over to the truck after everyone had gone and pulled a sack out from behind the seat.

"I got you something, Son," he said. "Try it on and see how it feels."

It was a baseball glove, the first I ever owned. There was something in the way he looked at me, grinning from ear to ear; a feeling came over me that he really cared about me. We didn't say much but I felt that he saw something in me that he liked, and that he bought the glove because of how he felt about me and for no other reason. It was a feeling I never forgot.

Soon after I began playing with the Coca Cola Travelers, we played Millington Naval Base at Toby Park, on the east side of Memphis. They prided themselves on having a good team. Many of our players had skirmished with them outside the ballpark, so tension was already running high. It came to a head in the seventh inning.

We were at bat. I was on at first and Bobby Wiginton was at

home plate when a hit-and-run play was called. I took off, and Wiginton hit a grounder to the shortstop off the side of his bat. The shortstop fielded the ball cleanly and got off a quick throw to second. Arriving at the same time as the ball, I slid in feet first to try to break up a double play, and the second baseman cleated me in the ankle. He obviously had meant to hurt me, and I came up seeing red. I clobbered him with a punch that caught his nose and upper lip.

The shortstop came running over, and I hit him too. By then I had really begun to enjoy the action, so when the left fielder came running up to defend his buddies, I laid him out. My own teammates didn't budge. They were looking out toward right field. The right fielder ran up about halfway to where I was and stopped. Then he turned around and trotted back to the outfield.

With three guys out cold on the ground around second base, the umpire sauntered out to me and in a kindly manner said, "Now, John, I am going to have to throw you out of this game, if that is all right." I offered no objection. Play resumed without me. When I returned to my team's bench, I asked my buddies, "How come you all didn't come out there to help me?" They shrugged indifferently. "We didn't think you needed us."

I was suspended and then was kicked out of the Park Commission League. But even worse, the day after the game was that second baseman's wedding day, and there he was with a broken nose and a lip that wouldn't close. His family was upset, naturally; even I could understand that. I heard they were going to file a lawsuit against me, but nothing ever came of it.

I eventually got reinstated in the league, due I am sure to Mr. Everitt.

But I no sooner got back in than I was in hot water again. I came up to bat with a couple of hits already under my belt, and the pitcher threw a high fastball inside the plate. I got out of the way, but as I jumped back, I thought, *this guy is throwing at me. If he does it again, I'll get him.* As he went into his next windup, I knew instinctively that I was about to be hit. He released the pitch, another fastball, and I saw it coming at me. I ducked just in time to feel it whoosh past my ear.

By the time the umpire bellowed, "Ball two," I had thrown my bat all the way across the infield, barely missing the pitcher's head. The ump jumped around in front of me yelling and screaming at me, and I grabbed him by the back of the neck and hung him up on a wire sticking out of the backstop.

I was thrown out of American Legion-sponsored play for the same kind of unrestrained belligerence. The game that did me in was between a couple of high school teams at Toby Park. A big, heavy-set boy on the opposing side hit a line drive over the center fielder's head. The score was close, and my first thought was that he was going to get an inside-the-park home run out of that hit. As he rounded first base, I gave him a little forearm shot that jolted him just enough to make him trip over second base and fall. When he got up, he came running back to hit me. He missed, and I punched him out right there. I was immediately ejected from the game. He was awarded a home run, which might have told me something had I been able to recognize poetic justice at that time.

I would not be surprised if I held the distinction of being thrown out of more ballparks in more leagues than any other player to ever play the game, but having Mr. Everitt for a friend assured me of playing in somebody's league. When I was thrown out of one, he immediately went to work to get me reinstated or into another. He taught me better than anyone else that the old squeeze play has its place no matter what game you're playing.

I worked during the summer months, but I tried to find jobs that would still leave me free to play baseball for Mr. Everitt. My friends worked too, and we managed to take every opportunity to drink and pull off crazy stunts right under everyone's nose. On one occasion, Jerry Reese and I were selling beer at a golf tournament at one of the country clubs. We had met at Memphis State University and played football there together, as well as baseball for Mr. Everitt. We started out by having a little nip every now and then ourselves. Pretty soon, it was more now than then, and by the time the day ended, we were drunk as cooties and twice as crazy.

We managed to get out to the park and into our uniforms for our ball game that night. Then we had our big inspiration. Jerry was going to play barefoot, and I would play shortstop with a catcher's mitt. I decided that playing barefoot was such a great idea, I would do that too. We were so drunk and crazy, I can't even remember how the night went, but we had a great time.

When I think back on my teen years in Memphis, I realize what an impact Mr. Everitt had on my life. Much of the success I enjoyed in college baseball and later with a professional club resulted indirectly from opportunities he gave me. He was truly a patient man.

After I married and went away to college, and even after I retired from professional football and came home to Memphis to stay, I kept in touch with Mr. Everitt. Once in an effort to show my appreciation, I took him out to a topless bar. I'm not sure what I expected from Mr. Everitt, but he didn't bat an eye—just sat there talking to me like he was accustomed to having females in varying degrees of undress parade past him. I have often wondered if he told his wife, Bennie, about that incident. If he had, I think Bennie would have killed me!

Unaccustomed to expressing my feelings to anyone, I could somehow talk with Mr. Everitt about the things that were important to me. Years after our baseball days together, I asked him, "Do you remember giving me that baseball glove?"

"Sure I do, Son. I didn't know how you would feel about me doing that, but I did it because I felt like you thought everybody was down on you. I wanted you to know I was for you a hundred percent."

"Oh, I knew that—all those times you stuck up for me—it's a wonder somebody didn't kill me."

5

In Pursuit of Freedom

Drinking, fighting, and running around looking for excitement was the life I wanted and lived as soon as I was able. Quiet entertainment was not for me. I liked being in a crowd and being noticed.

I had already learned not to depend on others to make my decisions, because I was the one who was going to suffer the consequences. When I asked my dad if I could go somewhere, anywhere, he had but one answer: "No." So, whenever I wanted to do something, I didn't ask. I just decided if I wanted to do it badly enough to pay the penalty; then I went ahead and did it.

There were no discussions of the teachings of Jesus in our home, but my dad always said a prayer before meals, during which we were required to keep perfectly quiet. The severity of the punishment when any of the house rules were broken seemed to me inconsistent with the basic notion of prayer. I remember during one of these prayers my little brother, Bobby, snickered aloud at something. Without pausing or lifting his head Dad backhanded Bobby across the face, knocking him back against the wall. This incident and others like it, caused me to hate everything associated with religion.

I went to church, though, but only because my parents expected me to. We always went on Sunday morning, Sunday evening, and again on Wednesday night. I memorized two verses of Scripture, and until I was 31 years old, they were the only two I knew. I could quote Hebrews 5:8, 9: "Though He were a Son, yet learned He obedience by the things which He suffered; and being made perfect, He became the author of eternal salvation unto all that obey Him."

At some point I was baptized, though I don't remember the exact date. We had a way of saying it, "b'p-tized," bearing down on that last syllable. If baptism was supposed to make me better, I often wonder what I might have been had I not been "b'p-tized." Since it had no real meaning for me at the time, I suppose I must have done it because I thought it was expected of me and would in some way win approval from my family.

In the latter part of my junior year in high school, my dad became ill with a heart condition and eventually had to be hospitalized. Because of the financial burden of his continuing care, my mother, Bobby, and I moved in with J.M. and his family. I found it hard to adjust to so much family under one roof, so I stayed over with a friend, Larry Sutton, most of the time. Larry and I ran around together, drinking and getting into fights. He was already out of school and working at Goldsmith's department store. I worked at various after-school jobs in order to pay my own living expenses.

One night while I was staying with Larry, we went out of town to a Frayser bowling alley. Frayser, a town in Shelby County, was not then a part of Memphis, so there was no city police force there. We knew a tough group of guys always ready for a fight hung out at the bowling alley. We decided, for that night, instead of fighting them we would team up with them and fight sailors and marines, who also hung out there. Soon after we got there, a big hassle began, with Larry and me in the middle of it. Immediately after the action started, I took a blow on the ear from a bowling ball that erased from my memory some of the details of the fracas, but it was a battle royal. Several guys were badly hurt, covered with blood. Suddenly the fighting stopped as abruptly as it began. The place was a wreck. Those who were still on their feet tried to act as if nothing unusual had happened. Suddenly Larry Sutton came charging down through the crowd whooping and hollering, and slugged a big marine in the jaw. That triggered another war!

Larry and I have remained good friends in all the years since then, and I often reflect on his loyalty to me in every situation.

Some of these clashes were just skirmishes for the sake of stirring up some excitement. Others, like the Frayser brawl, were more serious. One fight, the Humes Junior-Senior fight, was an annual event. We could have sold tickets to it if we had had any way of knowing when it would break out. Once a year, for no apparent reason, the eleventh and twelfth graders would start fighting in the halls. Once the fight ignited, everyone else would get out of the way of the flying fists until broken noses, black eyes, broken hands, missing teeth made it wear down. I couldn't wait to be properly qualified for that one; I liked a good fight, so I jumped into the junior-senior battles when I was still in the tenth grade.

I had begun to go out with girls, but when I wanted a date, I usually had to get out of my neighborhood because of my reputation for fighting. The girls who knew me were afraid to go out with me. If they had misgivings, I can imagine how their parents felt. In a crowd, if someone elbowed me or said something I didn't like, I'd start a fight.

Bobby Wiginton knew some girls who went to school at Central, and one night I was with him when we ran into them. Rita Rahm, who went to Humes High, was with them, and she introduced me to Nancy Andrews. I thought Nancy was the prettiest girl I had ever seen. She was tall, blond, blue-eyed—and very well built! I wanted to ask her out right then, but I was afraid she might have heard about my reputation.

I was impressed by more than just her looks; there was something different about her. She seemed sure of herself, as if she didn't feel that she had to prove anything to anyone. After I got home that night, I kept wondering what she would say if I asked her out. I didn't want to get turned down, so I came up with what I thought was a perfect way to avoid taking that chance. I called her up and tried to change my voice, pretending to be Wiginton.

When she answered the phone, I said, "Uh . . . hello. What're you doing, Nancy?"

"Nothing much. Who is this?"

"You know . . . saw you last night with Rita, remember?"

"Sure. I remember." She sounded cautious.

I cleared my throat and jumped right in. "I was just wondering what you thought about Bramlett."

"Who?"

"You know . . . the guy I was with. John Bramlett."

"Oh." She didn't say anything for a minute, and I began to think that maybe this was not one of my better ideas, and then she said, "I thought he was really nice."

"You did?" I hoped I had heard her right. I pressed my point. "Would you go out with him if he asked you?"

"I think I would," she answered right back, and I got off the phone because I thought she sounded like she was out of breath. I learned a long time later that it was not emotional excitement I was hearing. She recognized my voice and was trying to keep from laughing.

I didn't waste any time going to see her. I asked her to go to church with me on Sunday night. I tried to think of something about myself that might impress her; I couldn't think of much to talk about other than football. We didn't have much in common—we had different friends, went to different schools, and lived in different parts of the city. I had just made All-Memphis that year playing football, so I told her about that.

I think at first Nancy saw me as a challenge. She had heard stories about me, and she could see how wild I was. Somehow, that heightened her interest in me. I knew from the first date that she was the girl for me.

My home on Alabama Street and 686 North Hollywood, where Nancy lived, were miles apart in more ways than one. Getting there any time I would have liked was not easy, since I didn't own a car. I had to hitchhike or ride a bus. It was important to me for the Andrews family to have a good opinion of me, so Nancy and I did lots of churchgoing. Nancy's father was interested in sports, so I could talk easily to him. I was careful to present myself as advantageously as possible. Once when the Andrews were redecorating in their home, I went over and helped with painting and wallpapering.

I suppose Warren and Adelaide Andrews and Nancy's sister, Janet, assumed I was religious because I went to church regularly. They didn't know I usually stayed for a song or two, then slipped out and went down to the corner drug store to play pinball.

As regularly as I went to church, it still didn't bother me a bit to go out with a bunch of guys and throw brickbats indiscriminately through windows. Well, I guess there was some discrimination—I was extremely prejudiced against anyone who was different racially, which accounted for my choice of neighborhoods to harass!

The bitterness in me instigated senseless wrongdoing. I thought it was funny to walk up to a guy on the street, ask for a match, then when he was off guard, lay him out with a bottle or a stick. When I was angry, hurting people made me feel better. When someone tried to help me, I showed only indifference. Maybe it was fear that held me back from letting myself care— fear that by opening myself up to others, I could be hurt. Making myself insensitive to others was my defense against disappointment.

There is very little tenderness in the emotions of a man who will not allow himself to love. I had never known anyone like Nancy Andrews, and I was deeply infatuated with her. I didn't understand real love, but I knew I didn't want to lose Nancy.

I had high expectations for my senior year of school. *This is my year*, I thought; *if we can beat Central, we'll get some recognition and I'll be offered a college football scholarship. I'll have my chance to get out and be somebody.*

To my disappointment, twenty-eight boys came out for football, and only thirteen of them could play all the time. Bobby

Wiginton was our quarterback. Jimmy Alexander was a good all-around player. One of my best friends, Jerry Baskin, was a running back; Leon Weldon, another good friend, played fullback; Bobby Moore played center and linebacker. Jimmy Cruthirds was a running back. Larry Young, Jimmy Godwin, Larry Cox, and Donald Bennett all gave good effort; Bobby Biggs was small, but tough. He had an older brother, Ed, who was small, too, but the little guys just learned to try harder. I was light for a linebacker.

It seemed that every year, fall football practice got tougher. Coach Rube Boyce was a good, hard-nosed coach with great zeal. We started practicing long before the temperatures began to cool down; some days it must have been a hundred degrees in the shade. We had two practices a day with no water breaks. Afterward, we looked like racoons with our eyes peering out through layers of dirt and mud caked around our mouths. We couldn't wait to get out of those filthy, wet clothes, but we had to put them on again in the afternoon, and by then they smelled twice as bad. They were so stiff with sweat and dirt, they rubbed us raw. It helped if we could find a clean jock strap.

Central High was our arch rival. The school was located in a more affluent area than Humes. It was much larger and had a superior athletic program. They had no problem fielding two or three good teams, since almost a hundred boys came out for football. Because Humes was always the underdog, we harbored a deep resentment that kept us fired up to beat them. The rivalry never abated, but all the time I played football, we never won. We could play them a good first half, but with their depth, they always wore us down as the game went on.

One Friday night we were having our usual strong first half against them and were leading. It was a hot night early in the season, and I was playing middle linebacker. I'd been drinking and when I lined up at the start of the game, my stomach turned upside down. I vomited on everything close to me. Russ Vollmer, Central's quarterback, was across from me trying to call signals with his eyes glued to me. He looked confused, as if he didn't know if he should stop the game for me or go on playing.

In a pile-up, I managed to get my fingers inside Russ's face mask. I tried to rip his nostril open and was able to tear it enough on one side to start it bleeding. Underneath, when we wanted to get dirty, we'd bite, pull hair, scratch—anything to inflict pain. I always did as much damage as I could get away with. I was not entirely satisfied with what I had already done to Central's quarterback, so at the next opportunity, I stuck my fingers inside Russell's face mask again. Somehow, I missed his nose and got my fingers in his mouth. He clamped down on my hand with his teeth. There for a few seconds I wondered if I was going to come out of that game with all my fingers.

Over the years, Russell Vollmer and I became close friends, but in high school we were constantly competing against each other. In a mid-South relays meet, we were tied for second place in the 100-yard dash. The officials decided to break the tie by letting the two of us run again at the end of the track meet. Several heats had already been run; the last race was the mile relay. I was the kicker on the relay for Humes. This meant that I would have to run the 440 full speed, then compete with Russell in the 100-yard dash. After the mile relay, I would be allowed a five-minute rest before my race against Russell.

We learned later that during my five-minute rest, people in the stands were placing bets on the outcome of the race. A story circulated for years that while we were at the starting mark, I said to Russ, "If you don't let me win this race, I'm going to catch you out somewhere and whip you." A sore loser who thought I was too tired to run probably started it, and the way I ran the last 50 yards made it believable. At the 50-yard mark, Russ was 10 yards ahead of me. At the finish line, I had him by 5 yards.

6

Reaching for the Brass Ring

I have often wondered if my antagonistic perspective on life might have changed had I known early on that I would one day have the opportunity to play pro ball. But considering that when I reached the pros I changed for the worse, I doubt that it would have mattered.

By my senior year in high school, I had a distorted view of success. A part of my summertime work was taking tickets and ushering at Russwood Park for the Memphis Chicks. The Southern League was the big time for me; the Chicks were a great team. Showing people to their seats, then watching the game, was a thrill for me. Sitting there wearing the park's special sports coat and a tie, it was easy to dream of becoming a sports hero, but my dreams never extended beyond the Russwood Park boundaries. I would never have believed that one day I would get a chance to play baseball for the St. Louis Cardinals' organization—or football with the Denver Broncos, the Miami Dolphins, the New England Patriots, and the Atlanta Falcons. I had never even known a professional player; to me they existed only on television. Getting to dress up and rub elbows with the people who came to watch the Chicks gave my ego a terrific boost.

I got a lot of publicity throughout my senior year at Humes High because of my aggressiveness in sports. People usually say you should concentrate on one thing if you want to succeed. I wanted to do it all, and I wanted to do it better than it had ever been done. Experience taught me that it takes more than ambition to accomplish some goals. I played football and baseball, and I ran track. During baseball season, it was not unusual for me to play a game in the afternoon, then participate in a track meet that night.

A very close track meet taught me not to volunteer for events I knew nothing about. All we needed to win was to place in the pole vaulting competition. But we did not have a pole vaulter! Determined not to let first place slip away, I volunteered. I had never pole vaulted in my life; in fact, it always amazed me to see vaulters put a stick in the hole, go up in the air, and push themselves over the bar. Everyone knew that I'd try anything once, so they let me give it a shot.

On my first try, I hit the hole all right but about halfway up I stalled out, grabbed hold of a side bar, and rode it down. On my next try, I made it almost all the way up to the top before I came crashing down on my back. It knocked the breath out of me, but I wanted one more shot. On my last try, I went all the way up but grabbed the bar and brought it down with me. My efforts didn't count; even after that heroic performance we lost the track meet.

For me, 1959 was a fantastic year. In football, I had come from what seemed a no-win situation every year—cut up, banged up, too small, always trying to get a little extra out of my body—to making the All-Memphis, All-State, and All-West-Tennessee teams. And on top of that I got to play in the High School All-America game.

It was a dream fulfilled when colleges in Tennessee and Kentucky contacted me. I visited their campuses, but I was hoping for an offer from Memphis State University. When it came through, I already knew what I wanted to do. I went over to see Nancy and we made plans to get married. I graduated from high school in June and a month later, Nancy and I slipped out of Memphis to tie the knot.

We had heard that in Texarkana, Texas, there was no waiting period. We could get a license, take a blood test, and find a preacher or a justice of the peace to do the honors, all in one day. That sounded good to me because I knew Nancy's parents were not going to casually turn their young daughter's life over to someone without a job who was committed to a four-year agreement to play football. My brother Odell drove us the three hundred miles to Texarkana and helped us find a preacher to perform the brief ceremony. We were happy but all the way home, Nancy was very quiet, thinking no doubt of how she was going to break the news to her parents.

They were very gracious and compassionate. I am sure they were disappointed to have to give up many of their dreams for their daughter, but you would not have known by their attitude. Their kindness to me has never wavered. It was clear from the beginning that they would cause no friction between us. Both strongly believed in the permanency of marriage.

Three weeks after the wedding, I played in the High School All-America game in Baton Rouge, Louisiana. Many of the athletes who played impressively in that North-South game went on to make a name for themselves in football. Bill Battle went to the University of Alabama where he had a fine college career, then became the head coach of football at the University of Tennessee. Louis Guy made Ole Miss a great running back. A left-handed quarterback, Terry Baker, was outstanding for the North that day. He went on to Oregon State, and later won the Heisman Trophy. Lynn Amedee, one of the South's quarterbacks in the game, had a good career with LSU. The South won the game; Jackie Pope, halfback from Oak Ridge, Tennessee, clinched it by returning a punt to score a touchdown.

The week of practice was as important to the players as the outcome of the game. Coaches and scouts from colleges were there to watch and evaluate us. Compared to others, I was small, but I lined up against two big linemen in practice and fired out on them as if I were as big as they were. We had a drill of two on one. My best weapon was a strong forearm. Lined up against a six-foot-four Texan, I split his head open with a forearm shot.

My hitting got the scouts' attention, and I had coaches from Kentucky, Louisiana, and Florida talking to me. I told them I had signed with Memphis State, but I wasn't sure what the school authorities would say when they learned I had run off and gotten married. That brought a quick response from Memphis State.

Learning that these coaches wanted me, married or not, MSU representatives let me know that they would honor all agreements.

In August, Nancy and I moved into Vets Village near the MSU campus and set up housekeeping. Vets Village was a former army barrack that had been converted into tiny apartments. I had a four-year athletic scholarship, coupled with a burning desire to prove that I could play.

Nancy was young and inexperienced in the workplace, but she made up for any shortcomings in resourcefulness. She got a job as ROTC secretary to Colonel Gabe Hawkins, Air Science professor at MSU. We needed her monthly salary to supplement the fifty-five dollars my scholarship provided. I left it up to Nancy to juggle the funds to pay our thirty-five dollars rent and buy groceries.

The walls of our apartment were so thin that if you had private business to discuss, it was a good idea to go away from home to talk. Vets Village had few secrets. I learned how flimsy the walls were when one of the basketball players, Jim Dunavant, who lived next to us, came home after a bad golf game and threw his clubs in his closet. The clubs came all the way through his wall into my closet. I guess he put a little extra momentum into his toss.

Nancy's savvy as a decorator kept the apartment neat and attractive, but as time went by, it took all her skills to conceal the effects of my outlandish behavior. I'd come in drunk and knock holes in the walls. It was often carelessness, but if we were having an argument, which was not unusual, I sometimes took my frustrations out on the walls instead of Nancy. She redecorated every few months, taping over holes and hanging pictures to cover them. After four years in Apartment 13-A, we had some of the most unique wall arrangements you could imagine. Pictures were hung very high or at knee level, depending on where my fist happened to go through the wall.

In my mind, my four-year grant had very little to do with academics; I was there to play football. My major was industrial arts, my minor, history. I had no plans to concern myself with either. I made a commitment to go to class, so I did that. But my interest was in knocking heads. In our first game against Ole Miss in Oxford, Mississippi, mine almost got knocked off.

The Rebels were national champs that year for several good reasons: Ken Kirk, Marvin Terrell, Bobby Franklin, Bobby Crespino, not to mention All-American Charlie Flowers. Then there was Larry Grantham, who went on to stardom with the New York Jets. These guys were all on what was probably the finest team Ole Miss ever put on a playing field. They were big, which should have intimidated me, but I had always ignored size since I didn't have as much of it as I needed. I, a freshman guard weighing 163 pounds, went into that game against giants weighing 250 pounds.

They beat us 43–0, but the score was not what made the game memorable to me. About three minutes before the game ended, I hit Charlie Flowers full blast. His knee hit me in the temple and I went out like a light. I didn't even realize what happened. I don't know how I managed to dress myself and get on the bus to Memphis. I had played both offense and defense in the game against their big All-Americans, but it wasn't until I watched the game films that I knew what happened out on the field when 225-pound Charlie Flowers wiped me out completely.

After I got home, I was still so far out that I kept telling Nancy to turn off the television. She finally convinced me that the television was not even on.

Ole Miss was the arch rival of my entire college career. We would have given anything to beat them just once—but in the four years I played college ball, it didn't happen. The same kind of rivalry was carried on by the fans; they fought in the stands at every game. Every game ended in a ruckus between the players. If the final seconds ticked off without a fight, I could always think of a way to start one. We had a saying about our games with Ole Miss: "We may lose the game, but we wouldn't lose the fight." And we didn't lose many—fights, that is.

Soon after I got to MSU, I was confronted by my old nemesis, ROTC. I knew that sooner or later I would clash with those cocky student officers, and I'm sure Nancy was apprehensive about it. Working in the ROTC office, she probably went to her job every day wondering when I was going to do something to upset her bosses.

I hated to wear the uniform, so when I picked mine up, I decided to make it look as ridiculous as possible. I got my coat too big with the sleeves covering my hands, my pants so short they hit me above the ankles, and my hat several sizes too large so it would fall down on my ears. I went out on the parade grounds looking like a clown so often they put me in charge of the "goony squad." These were the troublemakers, of whom I was chief, and by removing us from their ranks, they could go on with their normal business without incident.

Having charge over the goony squad suited me just fine. Each morning I marched my squad across the field, down the railroad tracks to Southern Street, then up the street to a little café, The Campus Grill. By the time we had drunk a few beers, we would be due back at school, so we'd head briskly back down Southern, along the railroad tracks and across the parade ground to our classes.

I was constantly taking the heat from those student officers. It was "Mr. Bramlett, this . . . Mr. Bramlett, that," and depending upon the mood I was in, I sometimes wanted to punch them out. The simple "Yes sir, No sir" that they expected was hardly ever forthcoming from me, so I spent a great deal of time answering for it in Dean Robinson's office.

It helped my grades tremendously for Nancy to be working in the ROTC office. I coerced her into bringing me the exams so I could bone up on crucial questions, and as a result I made A's on most of the tests. That's about all I had going for me, and it wasn't legitimate. But because of the way I dressed and performed on the field, I still got D's as my final course grades.

On one occasion the ROTC was conducting a full dress parade on campus to honor the commander, Colonel Gabe Hawkins, who was leaving for a tour in Germany. My aversion to ceremony must have been affecting my usual sweet disposition because when one of the student officers, a sergeant, complained about my uniform, I was not congenial. I was picking up something off the ground with my back to the sergeant, and he kicked me in the rear. In a flash of temper, I knocked him cold. When I hit him, his nose spurted blood, and someone got excited and ran for help. Officers and instructors came running over, asking what was wrong with the man who was hurt. When I saw them coming, I stood the guy on his feet, then I stood there holding him up.

"What happened here?" the authorities asked. "What's wrong with this man?"

We were all conveniently vague. One of the guys finally mumbled, "Someone must have hit him and took off. I don't really know how it happened."

I was still holding him up. One of the instructors told me to let go of him. I did, and he fell back down on the ground. I'm sure they suspected me from the beginning, but it took them awhile to put it all together. After they got the facts straight, I had to go to Dean Robinson's office, and on to Coach Murphy's for one of his customary long speeches regarding my conduct. That poor man must have considered resigning many times during my four years with him. He wanted me on the team, but there had to be times when he thought how peaceful his life would be without having to contend with me.

In my sophomore year we had a game at the University of Southern Mississippi. Our team stayed at the Holiday Inn. Herb Anderton, one of our team supporters who often fed the players at his restaurants, got drunk with me while we were there. We went berserk and tore up the place. We went into rooms, spraying walls and people with fire extinguishers. I threw a chair through a wall. We threw furniture and people into the swimming pool.

Nobody knew for sure who created the ruckus, so Coach Murphy called a team meeting. Red-faced with anger, the coach yelled, "Who did it?" Silence.

"I'm going to ask this one more time, and I want an answer. "Who did it?" No answer.

"Fine," Coach Murphy continued, "The damage to this facility comes to $4,000. It has to be paid. You don't want to talk about it, so we won't talk. What you will do is pay for repairs to this motel. There will be no laundry checks issued to any of you until this bill is paid off."

We received laundry checks each month in the amount of $55 if married, $15 if single. I knew Coach Murphy meant what he said. My teammates needed their money, so I didn't have a choice. I went to him and came clean. "You don't need to hold the laundry checks, Coach," I told him. "I'm your man." Fortunately for me, the businessman who was involved paid the bill in full.

While I was attending MSU, I heard about a student aid program for football players which provided clothing and in one instance, a car. When I asked the coach about it, he looked at me in amazement. "Bramlett," he said, "how in the world could we ever be able to participate in a program like that with you around? It takes all of our money just to keep you out of trouble!"

Fred Moore was a good defensive tackle at MSU who later played professional ball in San Diego for five years. When he, Jerry Reese, and I got it in our heads to do something crazy, the higher the risk, the more determined we were to do it. One of our professors was out of town, so we decided to burglarize his house. We carefully planned the heist. Reese was to drive our getaway car. We gave him explicit instructions to wait for us at the corner with the motor running. When Fred and I got in the house, we couldn't find any money, so we poked around and gathered up all the cigarettes and beer we could find and made our exit. We ran down to the corner, but Reese was not there. We couldn't wait around holding our stolen loot, so we started walking, drinking our "hot" beer.

When we got back to the campus, we found old Jerry down at The Campus Grill, drinking beer with a bunch of guys. "You fool," I greeted him, "what do you think you're doing? Do you have any idea what time it is?"

He stared at us blankly. "What's wrong with you guys? What do you mean, what time is it? You got an appointment or something?"

"Naw," we told him, "but you did."

He stared at us with his mouth open. "Oh. No!" He sat there shaking his head. He had gone around the block after letting Fred and me out, had run into a couple of guys, and had forgotten all about us. Not the best man to depend on for a smooth getaway.

Off campus on Austin Peay Highway was a great place to go frog gigging. None of us relished the idea of getting down in the sloughs and ditches with the snakes, but we liked the frog legs enough to risk it. Pop Andrews (Nancy's dad) had given me an old 1950 Nash when I entered college. My buddies would pile into my car to go gigging. "Watch your feet, you jerks," I'd yell at them. "You're getting my floor mats dirty!"

I griped at the guys constantly about my car. If ever a vehicle could take punishment, it was the old Nash. So many people abused it, I don't know how it continued to run. All my friends borrowed it so often I sometimes had to wait for it to be returned so I could use it. One morning when it was missing, I went looking for Jerry Bell, a linebacker on the team who had borrowed it the night before.

"Did I have it?" he asked. "I rode home with someone last night." He had forgotten he took my car. It took us awhile to find it.

The old Nash was dilapidated with a bad list to the driver's side by the end of four years. I figured out why the driver's side was so bad; that was where the drunks took out their frustrations. When the driver got out, he gave it a lick with a forearm, or kicked it, maybe because it wasn't a fancier model. It did have one impressive distinguishing mark: a big eagle, poised for flight, which graced the hood with dignity. As much abuse as the car took, no one ever knocked the eagle off.

Reese, Fred, and I were out gigging one night and caught some enormous frogs. As usual, we were drinking. We thought it would be funny to tie a frog by his legs to the hood ornament. He looked so good squatting there, I had another idea. "Gimme a cigarette, Fred; this fellow wants to smoke." I stuck the lighted cigarette in the frog's mouth. Fred put a lighted cigarette in another frog's mouth and set him in the back seat. We jumped in the car and took off with our frogs puffing away. Every time they breathed, the cigarettes glowed and smoke curled up from them. We were all laughing so hard, I finally had to stop the car. I parked right in the middle of Poplar Street. We were just sitting there laughing like crazy when all of a sudden a police car pulled up beside us. Two policemen got out and walked over to us. One of them opened my door. "Just what do you think you're doing? You can't stop here."

I couldn't say a word. I just pointed at the frog on the hood.

"What's that?" The other cop walked to the front of the car for a closer look. He turned to say something to us and they both caught sight of the frog in the back seat puffing away. Those two policemen lost control. They laughed so hard they couldn't talk. When one of them was finally able to speak, he said, "Get that car off the street and go home!" Lucky for us that the cops enjoyed the joke so much! I took off before they could change their minds.

One night Jerry and I couldn't find Fred, so we took Jack Carter and James Earl Wright frog gigging. We went out to a lake and gave Jerry the light to hold. Right up against the bank we could see a big fish just beneath the surface of the water. Jack got his gig into the fish and brought it up, and there on the other end of it was a huge water moccasin with its mouth around the fish. We began jumping around, yelling at Jerry to hold the light steady. The snake was at least six feet long. It let go of the fish and fell to the ground. Jerry was trying to keep it in the circle of light when suddenly the snake came straight toward the light. Jerry let out a yell, dropped the light there in the grass with the snake, and took off running. He scrambled up the bank to the highway before he stopped. The rest of us were down there with the snake, afraid to reach for the light because we didn't know where the snake was.

I can't remember who got brave enough to grab the light, but we found the moccasin and killed it. After we calmed down, I had an idea how we could have some fun with our buddies back at the dorm.

I took the dead snake down through the dorm, and whenever I heard sounds from a room, I'd open the door and throw the snake in. All those guys sitting around talking went absolutely nuts. They were yelling and running over each other to get out of the rooms. I was looking for Fred Moore, who had missed our little party. He was in his room, stretched out on the bed sound asleep. I eased in and placed the snake on the bed beside him. Then I woke him up. He rolled over and his arm touched the snake. When he saw it, he jumped so high he almost hit the ceiling. It scared him so bad I thought he was going to pass out. When he realized it was all a joke, he started for me. I think if he could have caught me while he was that mad, he would have tried to kill me.

When I got home, Nancy said, "Elvis was looking for you. He called twice. I told him you would be late."

"Do you know what he wanted? I didn't know he was home."

"I think he was wanting you to get a bunch together to play touch football. He just said he wanted to see you while he's here."

"I'll call him tomorrow," I said.

"No, he said he would call back."

I think one reason those who knew Elvis best were never overawed by his fame was his lack of conceit. In those early years of his career, he seemed unchanged in personality from his Humes High days. We got together late the next evening and played touch football in Winchester Park. Elvis never cared what time it was; sometimes we played until two or three in the morning. One night we were playing at a school ground near his mansion. His bodyguards had a station wagon nearby with iced-down soft drinks for all of us. A big Cadillac limousine with blinds pulled down was parked off to one side. Elvis had a girl in the limo, but she didn't get out. After we played for awhile, Elvis went over to the limo and stayed with her for awhile. We sat around and waited till he got back, then we picked up where we had left off. It was fun to be with him again and hear him tell about all the places where he had performed.

He was fascinated by karate, and one night he invited a group of people out to Graceland to watch him and his sparring partner, Red West, demonstrate the martial arts. Red and Elvis had gone to Humes High together, and after Elvis became famous, he hired Red to be his chief bodyguard. When Elvis reached out to the people he grew up with, he seemed to be trying to escape the frenzied life that all his publicity forced on him. I guess he missed being an ordinary person who could do something just because he liked it.

He sometimes rented the Memphian Theater on Cooper Street to give his friends a private showing of the movies he liked, mostly old war movies and horror films. He especially liked George Raft movies. I think we must have watched every old black-and-white, George Raft movie ever made. Elvis even rented the fairgrounds a few times so he could take his friends there without being surrounded by crowds of people. It was fun at the time, but a long time later I thought about how important doing these things seemed to him. Fame robbed him of privacy and made him a victim of his own popularity.

One night we went over to play touch football, and Elvis came in with football helmets and jerseys for us to wear. He had the jerseys color-keyed so we could tell the teams apart. I laughed at him about the helmets. Only one of them had a face mask. He was involved in making movies and didn't want to risk getting his face messed up.

One of the last times Nancy and I were with Elvis without a crowd around was one Sunday afternoon when he invited us to Graceland for breakfast. It was three o'clock, and Nancy and I were eating breakfast for the second time that day, but it was fun to be with him. He always kept odd hours. Sometime that evening, Nancy went into the bathroom and found socks hanging over every available towel bar. She got such a kick out of it, she picked up a phone there in the bathroom and called her mother.

When Ad answered, Nancy said, "Mother, you will never guess where I'm calling from. Who is the most famous person you know who would have his socks hanging in the bathroom to dry?" Ad had no trouble guessing Elvis, and she had no problem with the socks, but one thing puzzled her. "Why on earth would he want a telephone in the bathroom?" she asked.

I drank booze wherever I could get it, but back in those days there was never any liquor around Graceland. Elvis served soft drinks and snacks. We just hung out talking sports, watching movies, and playing touch football.

I didn't see much of Elvis after I graduated from college, but I did happen to pull up beside him once in traffic. I had stopped for a red light, and I idly looked across the lane next to me. There was Elvis in an old blue van, disguised in a leather jacket and chauffeur's cap. I hollered at him, "Hey there, Man, how're you doin'?" He grinned, and hollered back, "Hi, Little Bramlett!" The light turned green and we took off.

When I was playing pro football for Miami, we played an exhibition game against Buffalo in Memphis, and I heard that Elvis came to town to see me play. Someone else told me later that he sat up in the press box that night and watched the game.

We were always hearing news about him, but because we had known him personally, his public life didn't seem quite real. Memphis loved Elvis, but it was more than affection, more than loyalty to a favorite son who made it big—it was wild, unrestrained passion and pride. People were emotionally caught up in his life. It was something he had no control over, as if he belonged to everybody else but himself. I reveled in his success because I knew where it all started. It proved to me that the brass ring was not so far away that it couldn't be reached from Alabama Street.

7

What Goes Around
Comes Around

The Golden Gloves competition was a prominent part of the
Memphis sports scene. One week, boxers would compete for the
South Memphis title at Gaston Community Center. The following
week, competition at Dave Wells Community Center would determine the North Memphis champions of the different divisions.
The third week, the winners from both North and South met at
the auditorium to battle it out for the city title.

Memphis made such a big hullabaloo over the Golden Gloves
that the football players got to talking about how funny it would
be if we could enter someone from Memphis State and win the
title. I was all for it; I had no idea that I was the one they had in
mind to climb into the ring against the fighter who had been
dominating the North Memphis bouts. Bill Crutchfield, a cab
driver, was six feet five and weighed 265 pounds. He was a good
boxer. I weighed 173 and knew absolutely nothing about competitive boxing, but my good buddies all seemed eager to sacrifice
me.

"You've fought all your life, Bramlett," they pointed out; "and
when did you ever get whipped?" I had to admit I had been
lucky. "But," I reminded them, "I am a street fighter. What do I
know about dancing around in a ring with gloves on?" (As a kid,
the one sports activity I was never allowed to participate in was
boxing. My parents were so opposed to it that I grew up without
ever putting on a pair of boxing gloves.)

"You'll learn. And we're gonna' help you get ready for it."

Yeah, I thought, *some help!*

I signed in as a novice heavyweight, which was at least half correct—I was a novice all right.

The night of the fight, the arena was packed. I felt pretty good. I had sparred with Jimmy Barnes, the North Memphis open heavyweight entry, a few nights earlier and came out smelling like a rose, which helped to build my confidence.

My match with Crutchfield lasted only three rounds, but the fighting went on awhile longer. My quickness kept my opponent from landing any damaging blows in the first round. I even got in a few glancing blows of my own, but my hands felt as if they were encased in balloons. In my corner at the bell I told Marty Grusin, my second, "Take these things off me so I can fight! I can't hit, all wrapped up like this."

"Just stay away from him. Stay clear and keep moving," he advised.

In the second round I decided to take things into my own hands. I kept moving, watching Crutchfield like a cat. Suddenly, I saw my chance. He dropped his guard, and I practically left my feet, slamming a right to the jaw. It rocked him off balance and into the ropes. As he bounced back, he caught me underneath his body, and we both went to the canvas. As we hit the floor, he slammed a knee into my groin.

My brother Charles charged through the ropes after Crutchfield, and about half the Memphis State football squad followed him. I was too busy handling things in my own defense to see what happened, but I heard later that there were more people inside the ring than there were outside. There was bedlam for awhile. When the officials finally got the crowd under control, we went one more round, and they awarded the decision to the cabbie. It was no great loss to me. I didn't see much chance of ever being able to adjust to that style of fighting.

The football team got together for a little powwow. We were not about to give up a shot at the title because of one setback, so we decided to enter two guys in the next South Memphis Golden Gloves tournament. If they both made it to the South championship, we would flip a coin to decide who would be eliminated and who would fight Crutchfield for the title. We convinced Richard Saccoccia and Jumbo Evans that they were big enough and tough enough to whip anybody in South Memphis. That was the easy part; they believed that already.

Richard won his first fight, but in his enthusiasm he broke a bone in his right hand, leaving Jumbo to defend our honor. He was equal to the challenge and won the South Memphis title, which put us in Ellis Auditorium for the city title match.

The night of the fight, I was in the corner as Jumbo's second. I had been his second all through the South Memphis fights. As a trainer, I was a joke. At the beginning, I took Jumbo and Richard out on the university's handball court to teach them how to spar. They went along with it because we had all talked so much, projecting ourselves as the tough guys. We now had to prove it! All of us had fighting experience, but not one of us knew anything about boxing as an art. And I, after having had gloves on once, was trying to teach the finesse of boxing to guys who knew only one way to fight: just slug it out.

Jumbo didn't really box that night. He spotted an opening and let go with a jolting blow. He made it look good for three rounds, and won the decision. Jumbo was the winner, and the Memphis State football team owned the Memphis Golden Gloves city championship. What a night!

I guess Nancy was bound to get pregnant while we were living in Vets Village. We were warned when we moved in that a more realistic name for the place was Fertile Valley. If a couple wanted babies, that was the place to go; the sound of crying babies echoed through the place day and night. I was happy when Nancy told me she was pregnant. I wanted a son who I could teach to be just like me. I was going to show him how to get the best of everything for himself, and that was going to be like me having it too.

Andy was born in July 1961, the year I turned twenty and Nancy was nineteen; our second son, Don, was born in October 1962. The day Andy was born was one of the longest of my life. An old friend from high school, Billy Chitwood, came out to the hospital and sat with me all day. Nancy had such a long, hard labor with Andy that I thought I knew what to expect when Don was born, but it didn't go quite the same. Forty-five minutes after I got her to the hospital, we were parents for the second time. We barely beat the stork there.

Dr. Turman came out of the delivery room with a big grin on his face. "Well, John," he said as casually as if he were commenting on the weather, "it's all over, Nancy's fine—and you have a beautiful little girl."

"A girl!" I blurted it out before I could stop myself. I hadn't even considered that possibility. I wanted another boy; in my mind the three of us were already playing ball together. "Well . . . okay," I said.

The doctor laughed. "John, it's a boy! And with the kind of lung power he has, if he doesn't make the football team, he can be a cheerleader."

"My boy won't be a cheerleader," I promised.

If anything on earth had the power to change me into a responsible, mature person, it would have been my two sons. I was proud of them and loved them, but I was the worst kind of example to them. Most of Nancy's help with the babies came from Pop and Ad.

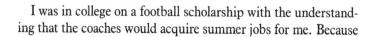

I was in college on a football scholarship with the understanding that the coaches would acquire summer jobs for me. Because of baseball and football, the jobs had to be the kind which allowed me playing time. The coaches wanted me to gain weight, so I expected jobs that wouldn't work me so hard. My first job killed that theory. At Kelloggs, I worked at what was called the tail-off. It involved standing out in the warehouse in the heat, lifting heavy boxes and placing them on pallets for eight hours at a hitch. After that, I went to a railroad car, where I unloaded raw materials, one-hundred-pound sacks of corn, for eight hours. At times, the temperature reached 150° in the box cars. On that job, I soon lost any weight I had gained.

My second summer while in college, I worked for the E. I. DuPont Company as a drum washer in the peroxide department. I wore a rubber suit for protection, with goggles and head gear on. With a constant flow of hot steam hitting me in the face, I was just hoping not to shrivel up completely.

It seemed that all the easy jobs like pushing a pencil or riding a tractor went to quarterbacks, running backs, and receivers. Russ Vollmer worked for a trucking line, but he didn't throw any freight on trucks—he sat in a cool office, working at a desk. James Earl Wright, MSU quarterback, was out on Jackson Avenue at Ford, in the parts department. He drove a tractor around, getting a good suntan.

There was one guy I wouldn't have traded jobs with. Dick Hudson, who later played offensive tackle with the Buffalo Bills for seven years, worked in the foundry for International Harvester. That had to be as hot and as hard as anything I did.

Coach Murphy must have considered a good day any twenty-four hour period when he didn't have to deal with some problem concerning me. In my junior year, the coaches recruited a freshman football player who was big and tall and a great prospect. He had been offered scholarships from 150 colleges but chose MSU after an all-out recruiting effort by the school. Their interest was justified. He was one of the first players from MSU to make All-American and went on to play offensive tackle for the Oakland Raiders, where he was All-Pro and had a ten-year career.

One of our unwritten laws on campus was that freshmen did

what the upperclassmen asked of them. One morning after football practice I was thirsty, so I told this new recruit to go get me a glass of Kool-Aid. With total indifference he said, "Go get your own Kool-Aid." I told him in detail what was going to happen to him if he didn't go get the Kool-Aid, and I warned him, "I don't intend to tell you again."

He didn't budge, so I doubled up my fist and dropped him. My fist landed right in his mouth and knocked out two or three teeth. One of the coaches grabbed me to keep me from kicking the kid in the face.

Coach Murphy sent for me. There in front of all the coaches, he read me the riot act.

"Bramlett, you've gone absolutely nuts! You're crazy! We've gone out after this boy, and after all kinds of trouble recruiting him and getting him to come here to help us have a winner—we finally got him, and now you're trying to run him off!"

"You're telling me that we're supposed to give this guy special treatment?"

Coach Murphy pointed a finger at me and said, "As far as I'm concerned, you're off this ball team right now."

I said, "Naw—you're not kicking me off the team. I quit!"

I left them all sitting there. I went down to the apartment and told Nancy, "Get everything packed. We're getting out of this place. We're leaving!"

This was nothing new to Nancy. She lived in turmoil from one day to the next, expecting the worst, I guess. Anyway, she knew it was pointless to argue. I am sure she never got used to the constant uproar, but I really never thought about it. I cared only about how it affected me.

Before we could pack and leave, the team captains came to see me. They had just left a meeting called by Coach Murphy in which my status with the team was discussed. There were many such meetings while I was at MSU. Coach Murphy was good to me, and I felt at times that he appreciated my enthusiasm. When we had a big game pending, he always looked to me to give a pep talk to fire up the players. When I did something outrageous, forcing him to take action, he always brought the whole team in on it. He actually wanted me to play, but he couldn't condone my troublemaking.

The team captains brought the good news that I could stay; they had voted me back on the team, as usual. I grudgingly agreed that I would stick around, after letting them know that I considered it very unfair for the coach to get so hot under the collar over what happened. A long time later, a friend told me the details of that team meeting. The coach had opened it with a little speech about me. He told the other coaches and players that he believed that unless I continued with the team and remained in school, I would be in prison somewhere within six months. He then said to them, "As far as I am concerned, Bramlett is through! He has been a disruptive influence the entire time he has been here. Had it not been for the reason I just gave you, I would have kicked him out a long time ago. I don't feel that I can support him, but I'm going to leave it with you. You make the decision. Take a vote. I will go along with whatever you decide."

Without any further discussion, my teammates made their decision. I am grateful for the unseen touch that impelled those players as they voted that day.

In less than six months I was back in the same kind of trouble. I was in the field house, playing basketball with a group of my football teammates. One of them began playing too aggressively. Jerry Reese warned the boy twice about elbowing when he rebounded, so when he ignored Jerry and elbowed me under the basket, I caught him by the arm. "Look, don't do that again. If you elbow me, I'm going to hurt you." He elbowed me again the next time we were under the basket. I jumped on him and began punching him in the face. I really hurt him. He spent a week in the hospital and almost lost an eye.

Every football game I played in was a big game to me, but the one most MSU fans remember best was our first win over a Southeastern Conference opponent in forty-one games. We beat Mississippi State University 28–7 after they came in a nine-point favorite. Russ Vollmer quarterbacked a great game; Dave Casinelli gained 154 yards in 32 carries. Bill Scott, John Cronin, and

Bob Finamore threw great blocks on the trap plays. Memphis State had 21 first downs to Mississippi States' 8, but we didn't score until late in the second quarter. They already had one touchdown—their only score of the game. Charley Killet dived in from the two yard line for our first touchdown. Walt Heitzenrater, Fred Moore, Jumbo Evans, and Richard Adragna played well. John Griffin had a good game too. I remember Russell Vollmer taking a kickoff to start the second half and running it from our own one-yard line to the Bulldog twenty-six. Six plays later, he went over for our second touchdown. Every player on our team felt like a star that day.

Our third touchdown came after I intercepted a pass on the forty-five yard line and ran it to the fifteen. Coach Murphy called it the key play of the game because it came while Mississippi State still had an opportunity to pull it out of the fire. It was just one of those days you don't mind having. . . .

After a ball game, my friends and I usually went out to eat and get drunk. One evening after a local game, two other guys and I went to The Gridiron on Highland Street. After a few beers, we got rowdy. We already had everyone's attention before we decided, instead of waiting to use the one restroom, we'd just go outside. We walked around to the side of the building where we still were publicly exposed, and relieved ourselves beside a window. Then we swaggered back inside.

A waitress saw this little episode and promptly called the cops. When they came, I started a rhubarb with them. They took us to the station and charged us with resisting arrest and indecent exposure. It always seemed to me that when I got into any kind of trouble, the situation got blown up into a lot more than I had in mind when I started it. While we were in jail, I began to sweat. This was my senior year and I was already walking a tightrope with school officials. They wouldn't hesitate to kick me out if the court found me guilty. So simple an act as a necessary bodily function was probably going to keep me from graduating.

The next morning, one of the other guys' employers bailed us out. I had not called Nancy; I knew she wouldn't come. She had already told me on several occasions, "I'll do anything for you—

but I won't get you out of jail." When the newspapers carried the story, using our names, Nancy went on about her business as if nothing had happened.

I showed up at my court date and denied everything. My two friends did not appear. I told the judge that I was there but was not involved in what happened, and he dropped the charges. My friends had forfeited their bail, choosing to look guilty to permit me to get out of it and go back to school.

❏   ❏   ❏

I wouldn't have admitted that I was seeking attention, but I got a great deal of it, both favorable and unfavorable. When the song "Big John" became popular, everyone called me "Big, Bad John," although my size didn't fit the lyrics. Early in my senior year, when the song first came out, one of the fraternity houses decorated a float for homecoming with an oversized figure of a football player on it, wearing my number, 64. They won the trophy for the best float, but after "Big John" blared out over loudspeakers all day and night, they didn't win any popularity polls. During football games, when I was on the field, the fans would chant, "Kill, Bramlett, kill!" The first time my mom heard it, she got really upset. She thought they were looking for someone to kill me!

Each year, the student body selected a Mr. Memphis State and a Miss Memphis State. Football players normally steered clear of all that commotion. Very few team members were in fraternities; we called them the "frat rats," and they usually controlled elections. They'd select a man from their own ranks, then organize an elaborate campaign. In 1963, my senior year, we decided it would be a big joke to run a football player for Mr. Memphis State. The guys picked me as their candidate, which really was a joke because the winner supposedly represented the school. Only outstanding people were eligible for this honor. I certainly didn't qualify scholastically, but since it was about the only thing I hadn't done, I went along with it.

The entire campaign turned out to be a positive experience for me. I had had a strong inferiority complex. I thought people looked down on me because I came from a poor family in a poor neighborhood. The chip on my shoulder was so big, I could never see any situation in its true light. After my teammates chose me to represent them in the Mr. Memphis State campaign, a funny thing happened. For the first time in my life, I began to take seriously the way others reacted to me. I had never been talkative. Suddenly, I was talking to people. I was polite and tried to be friendly to people I didn't know. Nancy encouraged me to give it my best shot.

The fraternities and sororities always had plenty of money behind their candidates; they put on a strong advertising campaign with posters, flags, and pennants. Football players never had any money, but I had another secret weapon. My good friend, Larry Sutton, worked at Goldsmith's in the display department. His ingenuity provided posters, banners, signs, and flyers, all promoting me as the next Mr. Memphis State. I learned to approach people and talk to them about supporting me, and of course all the football players were asking people to vote for me.

On election day, members of the team were stationed at all the voting machines on campus. When students came to vote, the guys very politely made their pitch for me. "Who are you voting for?" they'd ask. "Make sure you pull the lever for John Bramlett." Others, more diplomatic, made a little speech. "If you haven't voted, we will appreciate it if you will consider John Bramlett. As an independent, he represents every part of Memphis State, not just one select group."

Students stopped to discuss it, and probably more than a few changed their minds on the way to the polls. Surprisingly, I was elected Mr. Memphis State. The "frat rats" seemed slightly embarrassed after their six weeks of campaigning in which they didn't think I had a chance of winning.

When my picture came out in the MSU annual as Mr. Memphis State, it elevated my self-esteem. For the first time, I felt that people cared about me. It didn't change my mean disposition, and it didn't keep me from fighting at the drop of a pin, but I no longer felt like a nobody. For four years I had given MSU my loyalty on the football field and on the baseball diamond. I now felt that in a roundabout way, they had accepted me for myself.

I graduated from Memphis State University in May of 1963, with my BA in industrial arts and physical education. I have many good memories from my four years there, but some of my memories are also very painful.

8

Nancy

The part of my life I would like to avoid remembering in detail is the way I treated Nancy. I abused her physically, mentally, and emotionally. To relate all the details would probably hinder more than help the cause of this book. Let me simply say that I thank God that Nancy was able somehow to stay with me. I know it was God's grace that placed in her heart a love for me that never died through all those years of my faithless, unfeeling cruelties.

There were times when she was ready to pack up and leave. I don't know how she was able to look beyond the hopelessness of her situation, to hang on a little longer. I certainly gave her no reason to believe that I would ever change, but somehow, she believed I would one day. Occasionally, when I had humiliated her or had been uncommonly abusive, I'd say I was sorry, but after awhile I was not very convincing.

Nancy is strong-willed, with a determined optimism. She set herself to endure, and endure she did! When I made it so rough for her that she felt she couldn't go on, she would find a way to lift herself up one more time. Through it all she kept telling herself that some day it would be different.

I was drawn to Nancy from the day I met her. She was pretty, but I saw something deeper, an unforgettable quality. Today, she is more beautiful than ever. Dark blond hair that curled naturally and blue-gray eyes that looked directly at me knocked me out the first time I saw her.

She grew up in a home where all the right principles were taught. She had a legacy of love and responsibility that looked on the home as the best expression of the good life. To her, a home was where you brought your best. In the first years of our marriage, when things were really rough for her, she would hang another picture on the wall or make something pretty to use in the house. She loved beautiful things. That irritated me a lot because it reminded me that I couldn't give her the kind of life she had been accustomed to. I was the one it bothered, not Nancy. She accepted what we had and made the best of it. I am sure her parents' devotion to their home gave her a lot of her strength to stay with me.

Once when I had pulled some crazy stunt, she called her mother. Ad came over to our apartment at Vets Village and talked to us. She told Nancy that her place was with me. Neither she nor Pop believed in splitting up a home just because a couple had problems. Of course they didn't know nearly all their daughter was going through, but they wanted their grandsons to have two parents. They were like a second set of parents to Andy and Don.

Nancy made friends easily but didn't form any close friendships in the early years of our marriage, probably because she was never sure when I might embarrass her. One day on her way home from her mother's house, both babies were with her as she got caught in rush-hour traffic. Suddenly the cars stopped moving. Looking ahead, she could see what everyone had stopped to watch. In the middle of Broad Avenue, five blacks and a lone white man were carrying on a furious fist fight. As she got closer, Nancy could see that I was the white man. There were others fighting on the side of the street, but she was upset with only the one who had the traffic stopped. Luckily for all, the sound of approaching sirens dispersed the warring factions, and traffic moved on.

When I got home, Nancy shook her head and said, "I couldn't believe what I was seeing. John, don't you ever *think* before you get involved in such messes?"

The verbal abuse I heaped on Nancy never had quite the effect I expected. Something inside her refused to be completely dominated, or even intimidated for any length of time. I guess I would say she was cool under fire. And she was a fighter.

One of the times I got in jail, I called her to come downtown

and bail me out. When Nancy answered the phone, I told her
what I wanted. She didn't say anything.

"Did you hear what I said?" I asked her. "Come get me."

"I heard you. But I'm not coming."

I wasn't sure I'd heard her. "You can't come? What do you
mean, you can't come?"

"I didn't say I couldn't—I said, I'm not coming. You can stay
there in that place until you rot. I'm not coming." And with that,
she hung up the phone.

When I had angry fits and tore up things, she was sick about it,
and she let me know it. But then she would pick up the pieces and
go on as before. I remember once when I thought she was ready to
give up on me. I had humiliated her publicly, deliberately, and
afterward, she had nothing to say. I had never seen her like that
with the spirit gone out of her. Right then I felt bad about the way
I'd treated her. On the next day, looking straight into my eyes,
she said, "John, some day I am going to stop loving you." At that
moment, I breathed a sigh of relief. I never worried about "some
day."

Maybe every woman who has to live with an egotistical, overbearing man has to keep her own feelings on hold if she wants the
marriage to last—I don't know. I know Nancy did it. I think she
was able to convince herself that the mean streak in me was just
that—a mean streak that she would love right out of me. I may
have vaguely seen what she wanted from me, but I didn't know
how to define it and would never have known how to give it. My
background had not provided much affection.

I grew up developing the first law of survival: the ability to
isolate myself. I built a fence around myself, and the only change
I was going to make was to raise it higher. As time passed and the
mean streak in me broadened, Nancy had to learn to put up her
own fence. She held it together smoothly on the outside while she
adjusted to my moods and angry fits on the inside. I callously did
exactly as I pleased, daring her to cross me. I'm not sure how she
felt about that; I didn't want to know. I knew she was a good
person. I knew she loved me. She was generous; she cared about
people. As to what went on inside her to make her hold on to our

life together, I didn't care. I didn't even know that we had no real communication between us because I had never seen that kind of relationship.

Nancy is one of those women to whom motherhood comes naturally. After our son Andy was born in the summer before my junior year of college, she went back to her job in the ROTC office. We needed her salary. She didn't complain, but I knew she hated leaving her baby every day.

By the time she got her routine going smoothly, she was pregnant again. In October of my senior year at Memphis State, our son Don was born. She gave up her job and stayed at home with the boys for my remaining months of school. I enjoyed our babies, but the responsibility of meeting their needs was all Nancy's. I loved them as much as I knew how to love. (The one point on which Nancy and I were always compatible was concern for our sons.) Knowing how much they meant to me, she tried in my worst of times to shield the boys from what I did. She taught them to respect me when she could no longer do so herself.

Many times throughout our marriage Nancy had said, "John, if the bad times ever outweigh the good, I'm not going to stay with you." I didn't doubt it, so when I was especially mean to her, or if I stayed out two or three days without coming home, I'd go out and buy her a dozen red roses and put on my good behavior for a night.

Linda Parish became Nancy's closest friend after we bought our first home and moved around the corner from the Parish family. Paul Parish and I played football together at MSU. After we settled in Darlington Cove, the girls became a sort of "Lucy and Ethel" team. When one needed help, the other flew to the rescue, but you could never tell when one was going to help the situation or become a part of the problem. One week one would be in the desperate predicament; the next week it might be the other.

I'm sure it was apparent to Nancy in the early months of our marriage that she had chosen a hard bed in which to lie. Having chosen it, she was absolutely determined to make it work. Underneath all that outer softness had to be a core of unparalleled endurance.

It is hard to draw a word picture even of the one you know best. You can relate what they have done, and you know some vital facts about who they are, but because we all keep changing, the picture is never complete. It is Nancy's nature to look for the bright side. She could find something to laugh about most of the time, though a lot of that was for the boys' sake. Her hunger to make things better kept her from giving up on me.

Andy and Don have been blessed with a mother whose love has never failed them. If an issue is important to them, it becomes a priority to her. And she has given me that same loyalty during all the years I've known her. During the frustrations of my sports career, she could always find a way to challenge and support me, even though I'm certain she often wondered why.

After the boys grew up, I came home one day just as one of her friends arrived to visit. Nancy was on the phone having a spirited conversation with someone she obviously enjoyed. She was laughing and teasing, apparently having a great time at the caller's expense. After awhile, she reluctantly hung up.

"Who in the world was that?" her friend asked. "You sounded pretty sure of yourself there."

I had it figured out. "Let me guess," I said. "Which one was it, Andy or Don?" It was Don, calling from college.

I think it says a lot about the kind of woman she is that Nancy and her sons are very close friends. They can disagree without falling out—and she can advise without getting judgmental. She believes in people, and if they sometimes disappoint her, she refuses to become bitter about it.

I don't know if I have remembered to say how much fun she is. As you might have guessed, Nancy is my best friend. I not only love Nancy—I like her.

9

Just Call Me "Bull"

" 'I have had my mind set on baseball ever since I was in high school,' said John Bramlett yesterday after he signed a contract with the St. Louis Cardinals."

This quote from a Memphis newspaper was a joke. It was accurately reported; it just wasn't a completely honest statement on my part. Football was always my first choice because I liked the physical contact. I had been approached by several pro scouts, but disappointed in my size, they advised that I would fare better in baseball. "Not enough 'beef' for football," they said. So I decided to play baseball. I played college baseball, leading in hitting all four years. I had hit .323 as a freshman, .357 as a sophomore, .403 as a junior, and .358 the spring of my senior year.

The newspaper quote was a joke to my friends because they couldn't imagine me being serious about anything. The spring before graduation, in a game with Ole Miss, I showed them how serious I was. The baseball scouts all knew I could play ball, but they were leery of me because of my uncontrollable temper. The day we played Ole Miss, I knew Buddy Lewis, scout for the Cardinals, was going to be there to watch me play. I wanted to do well; I had high hopes that he could help me because he had previously signed Phil Gagliano and Tim McCarver, both Memphis boys who were already making noise in the big leagues.

The Ole Miss fans knew from previous games that I was hotheaded, so I knew they would be after me. But I knew Buddy would be watching for more than just playing skills, so no matter what happened, I was determined to remain calm.

From the first inning, the Ole Miss fans zeroed in on me, insulting me when I came up to bat. When I ignored their jeering remarks, they yelled obscenities about my wife and sons. For one day, Buddy Lewis saw me control my temper. I played the entire game without once glancing toward the stands, and I got that contract with the Cards. Buddy came to my home to sign me and to present me with an $8,000 bonus for signing.

I was sent immediately to Winnipeg, Canada, to join their Northern League farm club. When I left Memphis to start my professional career, Andy was almost two years old, and Don was eight months old. Our friends came with Nancy and the boys to see me off; Ad and Pop were there too. We were all so excited, we talked right through the departure of my scheduled flight, then had to wait around for me to catch a later one.

Vic Scott, a Memphis boy, was already in Winnipeg playing for the Cardinals. We hadn't known each other well before that, but it didn't take long for us to become buddies.

My teammates became well acquainted with me in my first ball game. When I came up to bat, I hit a double. The next man up hit a single to left field. I rounded third with Fred Koenig, manager, waving me in. I could see it was going to be a close play at the plate, so I came in hard, feet first, and barreled into the catcher. He went down with a broken jaw, broken nose, and some teeth knocked out. When it happened, his team came off the bench to get me. Vic was the only one of my teammates who came out to help me, but before it turned into a real brawl, those with cooler heads got it stopped. After that game, we were never able to play that team without fighting them.

Our team was called the Goldeyes. I think most of the Goldeyes were amazed at my ability to get things in an uproar so easily. With the exception of Vic and me, the Goldeyes were not enthusiastic about fighting.

Vic and I worked out a great pickoff play. I played third; he was the catcher. At a prearranged signal, I would sucker the runner into wandering off the base. Vic would fire the ball to me, inside third base. I would come up the line fast to catch the ball while throwing a forearm into the base runner, preventing his getting back to the base. The play worked most of the time, but it did cause some friction with opposing players. They always got upset and tried to start an argument about it.

The team spent long hours on buses traveling to places like Duluth, Minnesota, and Bismarck, North Dakota. To counteract the boredom, Vic and I would give the guys a hot-foot here and there after they fell asleep. We lit matches and stuck them in their shoe soles, and they would come up out of their seats yelling that the bus was on fire. We sometimes did that, too, setting fire to newspapers under the seats. As I think of those times, I wonder why Vic and I never seemed to require as much sleep as the other players. The Latins on our team all wore sunglasses on the bus, so we smeared shaving cream on their glasses. They slept for days on those buses, thinking it was still night, because when they opened their eyes, they couldn't see anything.

The people who came to watch the Goldeyes loved to watch me play. It excited them to see me run out on the field full speed and run off the field the same way. I put all the action I could into everything. Most of my sliding was head first. The fans liked hustle, and I hustled.

There was a rickety old wooden fence along the left field line of the Winnipeg ball park. During a game one day when I was play-ing third base, shaded toward short, someone hit a flyball down the left field line. I took off after it, running hard. I knew the fence was close, but I wasn't about to take my eyes off the ball. I went through the fence like a locomotive, but I had the ball in my glove. When I pulled back through the hole in the fence, my face and arms scratched and bleeding, with wood splinters hanging from my clothes, the people in the stands rose to their feet. Some-one yelled, "Look at the bull!" The crowd started chanting, "Bull! Bull! Bull!" After that, when I ran onto the field or came up to bat, the chant began. The newspapers picked up the story, and I became known as "Bull." The name stuck. The game that gave me my nickname also gave me my first home run in profes-sional play—a grand slam over the center field wall.

I thought the Canadians were great, although I didn't get along with them in the beer joints and on the streets late at night. One night, three of them started picking on me, and I jumped on all three of them. I had my hands full for awhile before settling things to my satisfaction. I got a cut over my eye in the fight—nothing serious.

On one of the road trips, Vic and I were staying on the eleventh floor of a hotel. Two pitchers, Charlie Haygood and Dave Guthrie, were rooming with us. I'm sure they did not choose to room with us, since most of the team tried to avoid us. Vic and I came in late, drinking heavily, to find Charlie and Dave already in bed. Charlie was scheduled to pitch the next day. I suggested going out for more booze, but Vic said it was past curfew and he was staying in. I slipped out alone and went down to the store on the corner. As I came back in I met our manager, Fred Koenig, in the hall.

"Where have you been, Bramlett?" he asked me. "It's getting late."

I said, "Yeah, I know it is. But I got hungry, and went out to get a few groceries. I'm on my way in right now."

I had a loaf of bread sticking out of the sack covering the beer bottles. He wasn't stupid, but he decided not to make an issue of it. When I reached the room, Vic and I started our second drinking party of the evening. I got to the point that I couldn't hold any more; as soon as I drank a beer, I'd throw up. Finally, it became too much for Charlie. He sat up on the side of the bed and said, "Bull, why don't you guys go to bed? We could all use the rest."

We got into a heated argument, and I got mad. I didn't want anybody telling me what to do. I drank one more beer and walked over to his bed. I asked him, "Have you noticed these windows?"

"What about them?" he asked.

"Well, for one thing, I don't see any screens on 'em," I said.

Both pitchers were griping about the noise and our staying up with all the lights on, and I was upset because they wouldn't shut up, so I said, "Vic, these guys don't like it here. Let's let 'em go where they can get some sleep."

Before they knew what was happening, I had grabbed Charlie and shoved him outside the window—eleven floors up. I was holding him by his feet, threatening to let go. Dave began yelling at me to hold on to Charlie, and Vic got scared. He started begging me to pull Charlie in. He was hollering, "'Bull,' it's a mile down there; don't let go, don't let go!" Charlie wasn't saying a word. I'm sure he thought it was all over for him. After a couple of minutes, I pulled him in.

Neither Charlie nor Dave mentioned again that night the drinking or the noise or the difficulty of trying to sleep with the lights on. I have often thought of that incident with overwhelming gratitude for the unrecognized power that kept me from dropping Charlie Haygood from the eleventh floor of a hotel in Duluth, Minnesota.

I was drinking and running at night, but still managing to play well. I was hitting the ball, and I was playing good defense. Toward the end of the season, the Cards club in Billings, Montana, needed a third baseman. They were in a tight race for the championship, so the management sent me to Billings. When I got there, I found a cheap little room to stay in when I wasn't playing ball or carousing. It wasn't much of a room, but I wasn't in it much. I spent my time off in a part of town I had been told to avoid. It was where the Indian people gathered to do their drinking and partying, and I liked it. I got into a few minor squabbles with them, but most of the time, we got along well. I missed Vic. I ran some with Cliff Polite, Ron Willis, who was from Memphis, and Larry Crayton, but I was usually the lone culprit in my types of entertainment and harassment.

Larry, whom we called "Pumpsie," was not a big man. When we went out together, he'd warn me, "If you start a fight, I'm going to be on the *other* side." One night he came looking for me after a bartender told him I'd left after drinking about twenty beers. When he found me, I was lying in the middle of the street on my back. Apparently, there was no traffic on the street at that hour.

I was glad to get that first year in baseball behind me. Back in Memphis for the off-season, I found a job with an insulation company and went immediately to work.

When spring training opened in Homestead, Florida, I was on the roster of the AAA Club Jacksonville Suns, under Harry "The

Hat" Walker's management. I did what I had to do to get in shape for the season, but I really saw spring training as a time for goofing off and having fun. The grueling daily routine came too soon for me. The teams had rooms at the various motels scattered around Homestead. My old buddy, Vic Scott, and I roomed together.

A young man with Memphis connections often came out to the park to watch us play. He was only sixteen, but he had wheels, which was a luxury I didn't have, so I asked him if he would take some of us around to various places after practice. The boy's father was a doctor. We used his car some of the time, although he was probably unaware of it.

One evening I had the kid pick me up, take me to a roadhouse of questionable reputation, and drop me off. I had never been there, it was out in the country, I had no idea of the location after I got there, and I had no way of getting back to my motel. Before the evening ended, I had occasion to reflect on the folly of my inattention to detail. As many places as I walked thoughtlessly into, I don't know why I didn't at least look around for an exit. Until that night, getting in was always my priority instead of getting out.

Not long after I arrived, the police raided the place. Three of the four officers rounded up everybody present while one stood in the doorway barring the entrance. I began to sweat. *This is going to be in the newspapers,* I thought. *The Cardinals' organization will hear about it. My family is going to find out that I am in this place of ill repute.*

I sat there watching the commotion going on around me, and I suddenly saw my chance. The huge cop who was guarding the door had turned away from the room to look out. In that instant, I charged him. I hit him in the back of the head, dived past him and ran full speed in pitch darkness, dodging shrubs and brush. I had no idea of direction. In my panic to escape, I didn't look for a road. I ended up in a wooded area, but before I slowed down, I hit a barbed wire fence. A jagged wire tore into me, and then I flipped straight up into the air and over the fence. I landed on my feet without slowing down. I knew I was bleeding, but by then I was hearing gun shots and sirens and lots of yelling. My clothes were ripped and I was scratched all over. I didn't want to get out of the protective screen the woods gave me, so I decided to risk being with the snakes and alligators rather than face those cops after what I had done to one of them.

I ran for awhile, stopping occasionally to listen for traffic sounds and police sirens. I could hear dogs barking; I couldn't be sure whether they were after me or were just disturbed by me. It took me all night to find my way back to my motel, but I eventually made it without getting caught.

My relief at getting out of that place was overwhelming. I had made it safely. I had some tall explaining to do the next day to my manager and the trainers. I know they didn't swallow all of my made-up story, but they doctored my cuts and dropped it. I played ball that week, joking about the close call I had, and bragging about giving the cops the slip.

One week later, Vic and I got our young friend to take us about fifteen miles down the road to a nightclub we had heard about. We got drunk and rowdy. I started talking to an army sergeant's girlfriend. When that seemed to irritate him, I couldn't resist seeing just how upset he could get. When he told me he was going out to his car for his gun and was going to blow my brains out, I taunted him.

"Go ahead," I said. "But when you come back in, you better pull the trigger or I'll take that gun away from you—and you won't like what I'll do with it."

I continued to needle him until he finally did go out. He came back and sat down with his girl. I couldn't let him get away with thinking he had intimidated me, so I went back over to his table. He ordered me to leave and threatened to shoot me, but before he could get his gun up, I blasted him so hard with my fist that it bent my class ring out of shape and almost tore the sergeant's nose off. I continued to hit him in the face. The sergeant's girlfriend jumped on my back, some other guys came in to help her, then Vic jumped in to help me. Before it was over, the place was in shambles.

We knew they would call the cops, so Vic, the kid, and I made a run for it. I knew I had messed up the sergeant's face, and we had broken up some of the furnishings, so we just wanted to get back to training camp without being stopped. We almost made it. But just as we were beginning to feel good about it and could almost see the lights of the training camp, the police pulled up beside us and motioned us to the side of the road. The two cops got out. One of them asked where we had been. I spoke up from the back seat with the first thought that came to my mind. "We've been to the dog tracks in Miami."

"Uh huh . . . I see." The cop turned the beam of his flashlight on my face. "What is that all over your face?"

I didn't realize that my face was bloody from the fight. "Oh, we play ball for the Cardinals down here at the training camp, and we've been out in the sun so much, I guess I got blistered."

He said, "Son, that is not a suntan I am seeing—that's blood. Get out of the car."

We piled in their car, and the driver took off down the road with his lights flashing. I was still thinking about how we could talk our way out of the situation when I saw where they were taking us. They pulled up beside three other police cars at the nightclub we had just wrecked and told me to get out of the car. When I stepped out into the light, a big cop jumped out of one of the cars and came running over yelling, "There's the rabbit! There's the rabbit!"

One look at him and I knew I was in trouble. This was the same cop I had hit and escaped from at the roadhouse one week earlier! He ran up with his gun out. Several of the cops grabbed my arms and handcuffed me, with my hands drawn up behind me.

The big cop placed his gun barrel at my temple and screamed, "Now, Rabbit, you dirty, low-down————, let's see you outrun this! Run! Run!"

He was almost out of control. I could feel the gun barrel shaking against my head. I wished somebody would get that gun before he pulled the trigger. He was ranting and raving, still cussing me, begging me to run. The other cops took me over to another car, probably to keep him from shooting me.

That night and all the next day and evening Vic, the boy, and I were kept in jail. The second morning, our young friend's father, the doctor, came and got the boy out, but no one came for Vic and me. The next day, Vic was released. After another day and night passed, I began to realize the seriousness of the charges. We had been in the doctor's car when we were arrested, and when the police searched the car, they found several kinds of drugs that were legal for the doctor to carry, but were illegal for us. I was promptly charged with contributing to the delinquency of a minor, peddling drugs, assault with a deadly weapon, being drunk and disorderly, and destruction of property.

The charge of assault with a deadly weapon was incorrect. They claimed I hit the army sergeant with a beer bottle, which I then broke and used to cut him, but that wasn't true. I hit him with my fist. But he was in the hospital and the important thing to the authorities was that they had the guy in jail who put him there.

I had joked about making fools of the cops, and seven days later one of them had nailed me. I sat there in jail cussing my luck. I could have used the time more profitably. I could have considered the fact that "God is not mocked: for whatsoever a man soweth, that shall he also reap."[1] I could have admitted that "the way of transgressors is hard."[2] I could have concluded that "there is a way which seemeth right unto a man, but the end thereof are the ways of death."[3] None of these thoughts occurred to me. I had never listened to the words of God—or of anyone else.

I did listen when Eddie Stanky, who was in charge of the Minor League system and in Homestead at that time, came to help me. After getting me out of jail, he talked to me at great length, giving the kind of talk I didn't want to hear. He had met Nancy in Winnipeg, so he began by telling me what a fine wife I had. Then he told me how grateful I should be to have a wife who cared about me and two sons who looked up to me. He said, "John, with them behind you, supporting you, I don't understand what causes you to do the things you do." He was a good man, trying to help me. I am sure it puzzled him that I could be so rotten and still have someone left who loved me.

Eddie explained my position with the authorities and with the ball club. As to the law, however, unless by some miracle we could get the charges dropped, I was going to do some time in prison. And my prospects with the Cardinals were not bright, even if all charges were dropped. The Cardinals were in the business of playing ball, not arbitrating my lawlessness.

I felt bad about the mess I had caused, mostly because of the way it could affect my future. Fortunately, we settled it out of court by paying the hospital bills for the sergeant and paying him a substantial amount of money.

Soon afterward, we broke camp and I was assigned to the Tulsa Oilers in the Texas League. It was a good club and I was happy to be in Tulsa, especially when I thought about how close I had come to playing behind a very high, very secure wall in Florida.

Grover Reisinger was the Oilers' manager, and I'm not sure he ever adjusted to me. He could get very emotional over little things like me calling him "Coach," which came naturally to me from my years of speaking in football terms. I guess I should have made a greater effort to call him "Skipper" or "Grover," like everybody else, but it did kind of liven things up to get him started jumping up and down yelling, "Don't call me Coach. Don't call me Coach!" I would smile and answer, "Okay, Coach," and he would go crazy. I could really upset him.

On our first road trip to San Antonio, we stayed in a nice hotel. In the hotel restaurant during our pre-game meal, I took out my partial dental plate and dropped it in my iced tea glass. I then called the waitress over. "Ma'am, I wish you would look in this glass. There is something in my tea." She took one look at the teeth in the bottom of the glass and let out a yell you could have heard a block away. We all enjoyed a good laugh, with maybe the exception of Grover.

After we got to the park, Grover herded us all into the clubhouse to go over the opposing lineup. It was all pretty dull, so I lay down on the floor in a G-string and took a nap. I don't think the players or coaches knew I was drunk. As I dozed off, I could hear Chris Krug saying, "Don't laugh at him—it just makes him worse." Chris said that a lot.

After a few months, Grover must have felt that he had served his time. I was optioned to Raleigh, North Carolina. Manager George Kissell must have wondered what he had done to antagonize the head office enough that they would send me to him. He was a strict disciplinarian and high strung, but I was glad to be there. My old drinking buddy, Vic Scott, had already been sent there.

Everything went fairly smooth for a few weeks. One night I had a few too many drinks before a game, but I was playing okay. We were several runs down until the eighth inning, when we came back with three or four hits and took the lead. That prompted George to send John Bukowski, his knuckle-ball pitcher, down to the bullpen to warm up. He sent me along with him. I was clowning around with Vic, who was going to catch the warmup pitches, when Cliff Polite came running down to tell me that I ought to be careful because I was making George nervous.

Vic hollered at me to throw him a ball. The pitchers kept a lead ball to toss from hand to hand for fast muscle loosening. It weighed eight pounds and was wrapped in white tape, looking much like a baseball, but not meant for throwing. When Vic called for a ball, I reached down and got the lead ball. I'll never understand why I did what I did next. I threw that eight-pound lead ball to Vic. It went right through his outstretched hand and smashed into his mouth, knocking out three of his front teeth. He was out cold, lying on the ground with blood pouring out of his mouth. George came racing down to the bullpen to see what was going on. No one else realized what I had done, so I said, "Oh, Bukowski threw one of his knuckle balls and Vic didn't see it."

After the excitement was over, I saw Cliff pick up the Pepsi cup I had left on a post by the bullpen bench, smell it, and empty it on the ground. He told me later that he was surprised to find that it was straight whiskey. Vic and I had been sharing it; I was surprised that there was any left.

Vic and I were always so hung over after Saturday night that we hated Sunday afternoon games. We were having a drink with Cliff Polite about one a.m. when Cliff said, "Hey, you guys, don't you think we better go in? We've got a double-header to-morrow."

I said, "No, we won't play tomorrow because we're going to get rained out."

"Come on, 'Bull,' there isn't a cloud in the sky," Cliff argued. "Let's go in."

Vic and I weren't ready to go, so Cliff left us there in the bar. The next morning the sun was shining and there was no threat of rain. When we got out to the park, George Kissell was already there frothing at the mouth. You could have rowed a boat around the infield. It was like a river. I eased over to Cliff and whispered, "See, I told you we were going to get rained out."

After Cliff had left us the night before, Vic and I had pulled all the water hoses onto the field and opened them up full. Then we sat there the rest of the night and watched them run.

While George was running around having a fit, we offered theories as to what could have happened. He finally decided that some local kids broke in during the night and turned on the water. He brought in a helicopter to try to dry out the field, but it had soaked up too much water to play that day. We didn't play ball until Monday night.

10

Benched—But Not for Good

The figure swinging slowly in the breeze was unmistakably George Kissell. It probably gave him a real jolt, but he hid it well. It isn't every day you turn a corner to find that someone has hung you in effigy. That alone could raise some doubts in your mind about your popularity. If George could have proven one-third of all the stuff he suspected I did, I would never have made it through the first month in the Carolina League. Vic was usually my partner in misconduct, though I won't insist that he take half the credit for inspiration. But he was always ready to jump in.

Riding the bus with us to Winston-Salem, North Carolina, where we often played, must have been a nightmare for George. Our infractions ranged from setting the bus on fire to cutting George's tires. One night I got everybody on the bus to join me in chirping like a chicken. We were cackling and crowing, getting louder and louder, and George stopped the bus. He made us all get off while he hopped around having a fit. I don't know what kind of salary the Cardinals paid the man, but he earned every penny of it.

Coco Laboy, who had been in Winnipeg with the Goldeyes the same time I was there, was already in Raleigh when I arrived. He was playing great, with 45 home runs. Coco was definitely not a hitter that pitchers made their living on. They had already started throwing at him some before the night we traveled to Rocky Mount, North Carolina, for a game.

At Rocky Mount, Coco was batting fourth and I was right behind him, batting fifth in the lineup. His first time up, the oppos-

Retiring of "Bull's"
University of Memphis Jersey, 2013

Don, "Bull," Andy

Hunter, Rachel, "Bull," Rebecca, Jordan

Darrell Waltrip, 3-time NASCAR Cup Series Champion, Daytona 500 Champion, Author, national television broadcaster, NASCAR Hall of Fame Inductee and Dear Friend and Brother in Christ.

Barrett Jones and "Bull," 4th grade Evangelical Christian School.

Barrett Jones and "Bull," 2012. All-American University of Alabama, NFL St. Louis Rams, Outstanding Athlete, and Dynamic Christian.

Andy, me, and Don. I've learned that a boy's strongest desire is to have his dad's love and approval. I'm thankful my boys never doubted my love for them.

Charles, Mom, Odell, (left to right) and me, in front.

"Bull" and Nancy.
God has blessed us with Family, Friends, and many wonderful years in Ministry.

My freshman year at Memphis State University. I had a four-year athletic scholarship and a burning desire to prove I could play.

Dr. Sonny Humphreys, presenting my diploma from Memphis State University in May 1963.

"Bull", Coach Tony Dungy (coach of the superbowl champions Indianapolis Colts), and Ken Whitten (pastor Idlewild Baptist Church - Tampa, Florida). Dear Brothers in the Lord.

"Bull" standing by his picture on the Denver Broncos Wall of Fame at the Denver Broncos Complex.

"Bull" and Joe Namath
Best Quarterback to ever play
Joe was Rookie of the Year in 1965 and I was Runner-Up.

Johnny Baker, All American Mississippi State, Former NFL star
Houston Oilers, Wonderful Friend and Encourager in my life.

I never went to the field without being willing to sacrifice my body. No one hates to lose, but I have always had a hard time believing that anyone hates to lose as much as I do.

The Miami Dolphins Bull takes on the New England Patriots (1968).

The Patriots Bull (1970) tackles Tucker Friedrickson of the New York Giants (left). Blocking a pass from the Redskins' Sonny Jourgenson (right).

Dr. Adrian Rogers - Always my Friend, my Pastor, my Hero.

"God is Love, and Jesus is Wonderful"

Coach Bobby Bowden (head coach of Florida State University) - a great coach, a great friend, and a great witness for Jesus Christ.

ing pitcher backed him off the plate with a fastball in, then threw
the next pitch straight at his head.

At Coco's next time at bat, he came over to the on-deck circle
where I was standing. Ever since I had been nicknamed "Bull,"
Coco and his Puerto Rican buddies had called me "Señor Bull."
Coco confided to me, "Señor Bull, I going to lay down a *bont*.
When I lay down a *bont*, down the first base line, the *peecher*, he
going to go over to *peek* it up, and when he do, I going to run over
him and hurt him bad. I do this, Señor Bull, because he throw at
my head the first time I was up."

Looking me straight in the eyes, he asked, "If I do this, will
you back me up and help me?"

I didn't hesitate. "Of course, Coco," I answered. "I sure will."

He walked slowly to the plate, took a long look back at me, and
laid his bunt perfectly down the first base line. As he ran down
the baseline, the pitcher came over as expected and picked up the
ball. As he came up with it, Coco hit him in the head with his bat.
The first baseman ran in to get Coco, but I got there first. Before
the first baseman saw me coming, I hit him. By then the second
baseman came charging in, and I hit him. With the pitcher on the
ground and the first and second basemen both in a heap beside
him, the manager went wild. He came running toward us. Vic
Scott intercepted him and bit off a big chunk of his ear.

Everything got completely out of control. People began fighting on the field and in the stands. It was one of those situations
where nobody seemed to know how to settle it down. The cops
arrested Coco, and that finally stopped it. After they took him off
to jail, the rest of the team waited in the bus for the manager to
arrange for his release. It took hours of negotiating; they had
charged Coco with assault with a deadly weapon. I haven't seen
Coco since that season in Raleigh, but I have kept up with him.
He went on with his professional career, playing third base for the
Expos in Montreal for several years.

When baseball season was over in 1964, Nancy and I packed
up and headed back to our apartment in Memphis. The boys
were happy to be with Pop and Ad again, and Nancy was looking

forward to the freedom of shopping and going places without having a three-year-old and a two-year-old in tow. I went to work in the Merchants Hotel Supply warehouse, and settled in to enjoy my free time in Memphis before spring training.

I liked the confident feeling it gave me to walk into a place and be recognized as one of the hometown boys who made good, and I looked forward to the time when the Cardinals would call me up to the team. I think I realized that I wasn't quite ready, but a ballplayer looks ahead toward the coming season as the best one, always thinking his next one will be better than the last. I was staying in shape. I stayed out late and did lots of drinking and running around, but I was working out and getting plenty of exercise.

About a month into the off-season, the ax fell. I got a letter from the Cardinals' head office. Its contents were blunt and decisive. Due to my undisciplined behavior and my inability to adapt to management, they could no longer use my services. The finality of the words left no margin for pleading my case. They were through with me. I was unmanageable.

It was not just a kick in the gut; it was an indescribable loss. Sports was what I lived for. It meant everything to me. It was my God. If I had been asked, "Bramlett, don't your wife and kids count?" I would have answered, "Sure, they do," but they were a part of things like ears on the sides of my head when I looked into a mirror. Sports was something I thought I could not live without. But now I was being forced to give it up.

Facing the end of my hopes for a career in sports was worse than any pain I had ever known. It was not the questions and humiliation of what I thought people would be saying that was tearing me up; I could handle that. I never cared what anyone thought anyway. And I knew I could find something I could do to support my family. *But I wanted my chance to play ball!* More than anything, I wanted to prove that I could go all the way to the big leagues. I couldn't deal with the fact that for me, it was all over.

I went to a liquor store, bought a pint of whiskey, and drove home. All I could think about was how it felt to watch a baseball leave the bat after a solid hit and keep on going all the way over the fence and into the upper stands. Anger that it could never happen again for me professionally kept building in me. The madder I got, the more I thought of the violent contact of football. I remembered the hard hitting in those MSU-Ole Miss games. When I reached home with that bottle of whiskey, I chug-a-lugged the whole pint.

I got so drunk and crazy I broke up the furniture, literally wrecking our apartment. I couldn't stop. I lined down in a three-point stance at the end wall of the living room and came up running. I went as fast as I could run straight into the wall of the kitchen and right through it. My head and shoulders came out on the kitchen side, with broken plaster and wood falling all around me. When I sobered up, I saw how close I came to breaking my neck. My head had missed a two-by-four by about an inch.

Nancy, always a fighter, was never one to run when it got tough in the trenches. If anyone understood the frustration of trying to cope with my rebelliousness, it was Nancy. She could have pointed out to me the hard, cold facts of how I brought myself down. She didn't. She encouraged me to stay in touch with the sports people I knew. We heard that Eddie Stanky had gone to work for the Mets, and Nancy said, "You ought to talk to him. I wonder what he would say if he knew you wanted to get back into baseball." She wouldn't let the subject of getting back in sports die. "Stay in shape," she said. "For all you know, some NFL football team may get desperate for a linebacker."

It took her about two days to remind me that when your game plan fails to move the ball, you don't cancel the game and go home. I contacted Eddie Stanky. He was cautious, but not pessimistic. "I will look into our situation here," he said, "and do what I can for you."

After all the trouble I had given him, his promise to try to help me really encouraged me. It soothed a lot of my anger. I didn't go so far as to blame myself for what had happened, but I did admit a grudging respect for the Cards, and I did appreciate the chance they had given me to play. I appreciated those in the organization who had looked the other way when I messed up, and I assured Eddie Stanky that I would not blow another chance. I said, "Mr.

Stanky, if the Mets can use me, I will see that they are never sorry."

Two days later I received a call from Denver, Colorado. Ray Malavasi was on the line. When he began talking about football, I thought, *Maybe there's a chance for me yet.* As Ray talked to me about starting a weight program and explained how the various methods of weight lifting could increase my size and strength, I got excited. At a low point in my life, he gave me the motivation I needed. I had not thought of failing. If this man believed in me enough to use his influence to help me, I owed it to him to prove him right.

As I look back on what seemed an impossible goal of putting on enough weight while getting in shape to try out for the Broncos by the time their training camp opened, it amazes me that I overlooked the most rewarding phase of the work. From late fall to early spring, I did not drink, smoke, or chew. I went to bed at night. I felt better physically than at any other time in my life. I suppose I attributed the great feeling to my hopes of playing football again.

The unusual calm in our home throughout that time must have confused Andy and Don. For the first time in their lives, I sat at the table with them for every meal and was home with them every night. Had my motivation been right, I'm sure my whole life would have become quite different. I know that many of the people I hurt would see me in a different light today.

At the end of the six months' self-disciplined concentration, I was ready. As I waved goodbye to Nancy and the boys at the airport in Memphis, I had never felt so good about myself.

When I got off the plane in Denver, I promised myself that I was going to wear that Bronco uniform—and I was going to have everything I ever wanted. The Bull was ready to break out. . . . I wasn't going to live my life on the bench.

11

Bull Out of the Pen—Again

The first regular season pro football game of 1965 was on a miserable day in Denver. Rain had fallen intermittently all week. On Sunday morning, a cold wind blew in, making it even more unpleasant. I hardly noticed. I had survived the Broncos' training camp. I had earned Coach Speedie's grudging approval after my initial roughing up his receivers and running backs had angered him. I was a Bronco, on my first day of doing what I loved best, and it was going to take a lot more than rain to dampen my spirits. Our promotion director, Jerry Fay, had the locker room doors labeled "Chute No. 1, Broncos' Corral," and "Chute No. 2, Visitors' Corral." When I saw the lettering, I couldn't wipe the grin off my face as I mentally changed Chute No. 1 to read "Bramlett's Corral."

The start of the game was delayed seven minutes because of traffic snarls outside Mile High Stadium. That game with the Buffalo Bills drew the largest crowd ever to see a Denver home-opener. The 30,682 fans more than doubled the attendance figure of the year before.

It was not a well-executed game. The field was slippery underfoot. Jack Kemp, quarterback for Buffalo, and our quarterback, Mickey Slaughter, threw 91 passes in the game for a total of 567 yards. All my concentration was on doing my part to make it a memorable game. I was maligned a little by the Bills for over-enthusiasm, drawing a few penalties for delicate infractions like piling on and tackling out of bounds, but Haygood Clark, who stole a Slaughter pass to set up one of their scores, defended me. His quote in *The Denver Post* next day, "a tough linebacker like

101

Bramlett is just naturally going to run over people," took the sting out of the penalties. Game statistics were fairly close, but Buffalo won 30–15.

Two of my big games that first year were played against the Chargers in Denver and the Oilers in Houston. We lost the one against the Chargers in the final minutes. The score was tied late in the fourth quarter, 21–21. On third down, the Broncos had the ball on the three-yard line. Cookie Gilchrist dropped John McCormick's pass in the end zone, then Gary Kroner sliced his short field goal attempt wide of the goal posts.

One thing you can count on in football is that the same miscue that takes the steam out of a team has the reverse effect on the opposing players. San Diego got so fired up after we came away with nothing on that drive that they scored two quick touchdowns. They beat us 35–21.

We had come from behind twice to tie the score on a league-leading, highly-favored team with such veteran players as John Hadl, Paul Lowe, and Lance Alworth, but that was small consolation to me. I had played all-out, and felt good about my game. I threw Hadl for losses of four and fifteen yards, and I blocked a Chargers' field goal attempt from the thirty-eight yard line. I had six outright tackles and five assists in the game. On one play, I was so anxious to stop Alworth that I failed to observe the out-of-bounds stripe. I hit him off the field and got a fifteen-yard penalty. After that, I was more careful, remembering a college game when I drew three consecutive fifteen yard penalties for similar infractions.

In my sophomore year, I had given Ole Miss forty-five yards in three plays, taking them from mid-field to the five yard line all by myself. MSU Coach "Spook" Murphy grabbed my arm and exploded on the sideline: "Bramlett, what are you trying to do? You're gift wrapping this game for them! Who are you playing for?" I could only nod sheepishly. "I know, Coach; I know. But I'll get it back. And I'll be careful how I hit 'em. I'll learn." He just shook his head with a pained look on his face.

But that memory flash didn't keep me from making a diving tackle on Paul Lowe at the nine yard line to save a touchdown. He ran the ball thirty-three yards before I caught him and flattened him. No penalty came this time, however, and Ray Malavasi called me over after the play and said, "Keep on hitting 'em!" It didn't change the game's outcome; the Chargers still came out on top.

Later that week, I was invited to speak at the Broncos Quarterback Club, and I took advantage of the opportunity to share a little southern style humor with the press. My reviews in the Denver papers suggested I may have missed my calling. Harry Farrar's *Sports Diary* stated:

> Last Sunday's disaster was forgiven when Bramlett, *Bronco of the Week*, choked the microphone into submission and went into a burlesque act that somehow got past the BQC censor. It is a mystery to me, a refugee from the Confederacy, why a cornpone accent is so outrageously funny, but the folks just about blew out their laughter tubes when Bramlett performed a modified Dizzy Dean number. Bramlett is a bonafide southern entertainer, hailing from Memphis. If he had sung "Wabash Cannonball," he would probably still be at the mike doing encores.

Shoot, I was just trying to put everyone in a good mood before the game films were shown, which I didn't hang around to watch. No amount of editing was going to change the score.

We were hoping for a two-game sweep with Houston the following week. We had beaten them earlier in the season in Denver but we had never won in Houston. After that November 14th game, the Oilers' quarterback, George Blanda, must have thought a hex had fallen on him. In our two games with them in 1965, we picked off eleven of his passes. In all his other games combined, he had thrown only nine interceptions.

The game began with the old pro, Blanda, going sixty-seven yards in six plays, connecting on his first of three conversions. The game was only four minutes old when he threw a scoring strike to Charley Frazier. The Broncos couldn't tally. An exchange of interceptions helped Houston to its second touchdown. Weak safety Goose Gonsoulin took one away from Blanda, but seconds later quarterback McCormick lobbed one up that Houston's Bobby Maples, linebacker, picked off on a diving catch.

Blanda passed to runningback Ode Burrell from twelve yards out for the second touchdown.

With eight seconds to go in the second quarter, McCormick notched a completion to flanker Lionel Taylor for Denver's first score. Kicker Kroner's conversion made it 14–7. Things really got wild after that. Bronco receivers were dropping passes; several were overthrown. It was going poorly for us offensively, so we changed our defensive tactics. We doubled coverage of their pass receivers and began zoning more on defense. Houston players began tipping passes, and we intercepted them. We took six away from Blanda in that game. In the third quarter, we finally tied the score. In the fourth our punter, Bob Scarpitto, boomed a sixty-four yarder out of bounds on Houston's one yard line. After gaining only two yards, the Oilers punted, and Abner Haynes, Denver's halfback, went fifty-seven yards to score. After that, the Oilers never caught us.

I played with a hurt shoulder, but I had a good day. With less than two minutes left in the game, Blanda fired the ball to Frazier on first down and I was laying off in the flat waiting for it. I ran twenty-five yards for the touchdown, which sealed the verdict. It was a thrill to intercept and score like that. I had always said, "If I ever get to have a play like that, I'm going to throw the ball into the stands." My injured shoulder was so sore that I couldn't lift my arm to throw, so I punted the ball as high as I could straight up in the air. It came down where the umpire stood waiting for us to go for the extra point. He caught it and set it down at his feet. The crowd gave me a standing ovation.

The final score was 31–21. It was our first victory in American Football League history in Houston. The game ball was given to the defense, which made me proud. "How sweet it is," defensive coach George Dickson laughed as he accepted it. We didn't escape unscathed. Jerry Hopkins, a third-year linebacker, had surgery the following week to repair torn cartilage in a knee; Ray Jacobs and Charlie Janerette, defensive tackles, both suffered leg injuries. Max Leetzow, rookie defensive end, sprained an ankle. And the game didn't help my shoulder injury any. We had already lost our premier quarterback, Slaughter, early in the season.

But that particular game was our best team effort all season. John Griffin, Cookie Gilchrist, Darrel Lester, and Nemiah Wilson all had a great game. I was just glad to squeak by without getting a penalty called on me. In our first game with Houston, Jack Spikes had gotten me penalized fifteen yards by insisting I bit him. I'd worn an upper denture plate since high school, so I couldn't have bitten him if I had tried. In order to play I had to wear a rubber mouthpiece to prevent my teeth from going through my gums. All through that game, the Houston coach kept yelling to the officials from the sidelines, "Get that Bramlett! He hasn't made a legal tackle all day!" They tacked about seventy-five yards in penalties on me, but I contested the one about biting. I ran right up to the ref and showed him my gums. He just looked at me and said, "Oh . . . I'm sorry, son," then went right on stepping off the fifteen yards against me.

After our game in Houston, John McCormick, who did not have his best day passing the ball, summed it all up. "It wasn't the prettiest way to win," he said, "but we'll take it!"

Waking up on Monday morning after a hard game was torture of the worst kind. After I got several injuries, I went into every game shot full of novacaine, cortizone, and some drugs I can't even remember. As soon as the game ended, I always started drowning my pain in whiskey. All that booze and drugs mixed together made me so crazy I didn't know or care what I was doing much of the time. Nancy spent a lot of time that first year talking to Allen Hurst, the team trainer. She was always looking for a way to make things easier for me. She ignored the wild things I did off the field. I played with injuries which should have kept me on the bench, and when the games were over, I had to be patched up just to get home. Returning home from an away game, it was not uncommon for me to hobble on board the plane on crutches.

Before games, Nancy, with tears running down her face, would plead with me, "John, you've got to tell them how you're hurting." I'd just shake my head and growl, "I gotta' go." I had felt driven all my life; whatever it was, it still drove me. I couldn't let up.

The Denver newspapers gave wide coverage to my all-out style of playing. "Hey, look here," I told Charlie Parker one day. "Read this. I have grown two inches taller and gotten twenty pounds heavier since yesterday's game."

"Call 'em up," Charlie said. "Tell 'em you just look that way because you're *all bull*." He grinned. "Hey, Bull—maybe that writer got his info from quarterbacks. You probably look that big to them."

I did like to blitz quarterbacks. The *Denver Post* sports editor noted that if I were a pilot during a war, I would have pictures of at least seven top quarterbacks painted on my fuselage. I had tackled them all for long losses: Babe Parelli (Patriots), Joe Namath (Jets), Pete Beatherd (Chiefs), George Blanda (Oilers), Jack Kemp (Bills), John Hadl (Chargers), and Mike Taliaferro (Jets). I was trying to make sure they would look for me the next time around. . . .

All my life, my heroes had been the tough guys, the ones who never quit. From high school on, my idol was Sam Huff, middle linebacker for the New York Giants. In the fifties, the Giants won the NFL Eastern Division title three times, with Sam a great contributing factor. I wanted to be the same kind of player— dedicated, tough, and smart. The kind of player you may be able to fool once, but never more than once. A few of the players I had played against were like that.

I went home one day to see Nancy standing in the doorway reading a newspaper. She held it out to me. "Before you read that," she said, "who do you say is the toughest man you have played against?" "That's easy," I answered. "Mack Lee Hill. He's the best." Mack was a Kansas City fullback.

"I thought that was who you would say. You'll hate this. Mack Lee Hill is dead. He died on the operating table during surgery."

I felt really bad about it, not only for his family and the Chiefs, but because I admired the kind of player he was. When you went for him, you were going to need extra help. That was the kind of strength and the kind of player I respected.

One of the great memories of my professional career came after the first season ended. At an All-Sports Award Banquet, Curtis Person, Sr., and I were honored as the city's best amateur and professional athletes of the year, Curtis as an amateur golfer of national reputation, and I as a pro football player. The event was held in the Mid-South Coliseum, with about six hundred guests present. Sports figures I knew and admired were there: Jim Taylor, Green Bay Packer fullback, and Phil Gagliano and Tim McCarver of the baseball St. Louis Cardinals.

After we got home that night, Nancy asked, "Well, how does it feel to be introduced as the best linebacker in football?"

"Don't you think Billy Murphy and Ray Malavasi both got kinda' carried away?" I asked.

"No," she argued. "I didn't think they exaggerated. They showed the film footage to back it up. Well, I guess they stretched it a little about you being a self-made man. And, you may have noticed who Ray credited with your success!" She drew herself up and tried to imitate Malavasi's voice: "Let's give credit where it is due. John's wife, Nancy, had more to do with his success than anybody else."

"Knock it off," I said. "I know who had to crawl off that field after a hard game. I know who took those licks."

At the banquet when I said, "It is a great thrill to me to be recognized in this way by my home town—it is a high point of my life," I meant every word of it. It was a great night!

Dixiemart Corondolet offered me a job during the off-season as their consultant for uniforms and for baseball, softball, basketball, or football equipment. Michael Lynn, store manager, made it enjoyable work for me by encouraging kids who were interested in sports to come by to talk to me. I'd answer their questions and sign autographs. Michael Lynn has since become General Manager for the Minnesota Vikings.

Several well-known sports personalities played in that year's Pro-Am Golf Tournament in Memphis. Joe Namath accepted an invitation and brought with him his lawyer, Mike Bike. I followed Joe around Colonial Country Club's course, kidding him about his game and talking football. Nancy and the boys came out and met Joe and Mike, and we all went over to visit with Pop and Ad. Before leaving Memphis, Joe had Nancy's promise to cook Southern-fried chicken, hot biscuits, and gravy for him on his next trip to Denver to play ball. He was the kind of person who made us feel right away that we were old friends.

Before summer's end I was anxious to get back to Denver. I was a familiar figure in the joints of both Memphis and Denver. Action after hours was the same for me wherever I was. I could go for days on a few hours of sleep, drinking and popping pills. I had recovered well from my injuries of the previous season and was ready to play football. The violence of the game was something I had conditioned myself to, and anything less left me feeling frustrated and restless.

12

Putting It All on the Line

Before my second season as a Bronco, I signed a contract that doubled my first year's salary. It still was peanuts compared to others in my situation, but I loved the game and wasn't greedy. I never had an agent, and I never was a hold-out. My way of dealing with management was to negotiate an agreement as fairly and as quickly as possible, then get on with the game.

Excited about the 1966 season, I was ready to start knocking heads together. In our first regular season game, I was running across the field to tackle Ode Burrell, Houston running back, when he cut back against the flow. I threw my body in an effort to catch him, and when I came down, my shoulder hit the ground in a twist. Taking the blow in that unnatural position tore every small muscle that attaches to the big central shoulder muscle completely loose. All of the small muscles unravelled down my back.

I was in intense pain, but after being shot up with novacaine and cortizone, I went back in and played the entire game. For the rest of the season, I was unable to lift my arm above my head. The doctors never could find the cause of the trouble, so after checking me out, they'd shoot cortizone into my shoulder and let me go. Because I had learned to play with painful injuries, no one knew how serious this one actually was. I played every game with my shoulder tightly taped to my body so I could still throw a forearm into a player. After the season ended, I played in the Pro Bowl while ignoring the pain in my torn-up left shoulder.

I had a good year in '66 in spite of my injury. In a game with the Kansas City Chiefs, I broke up a pass from quarterback Len Dawson to flanker Chris Burford which could have been a touchdown play for us if I had been able to lift my left arm to catch the ball. Instead of making the interception, I jumped in front of Burford and knocked the ball to the ground. The Chiefs won the game, but not before we got their attention with our specialty team's play.

Late in the game, I kayoed Mike Garrett along the sideline in a tackle that aroused Hank Stram's ire. Garrett, Heisman Trophy winner from Southern Cal, was a rookie running back for the Chiefs. When he came to my side on a sweep, with a blocker all over me, my only shot was to clothesline him by swinging my outstretched right arm across his face. The hit busted his face mask and knocked him out cold, right in front of the Kansas City bench. The Chiefs who were standing on the sideline began throwing buckets of ice on me, and Coach Stram was screaming his head off at me and at the officials. I thought the hit was fair. Hard, but fair. Stram didn't agree. He immediately called Dawson over to the side and gave him a play designed just for me.

We were on the hashmark closest to their bench, so they ran a sweep away from me. They handed off the ball to a running back, sending him wide to the other side of the field. When all my teammates went for the ball carrier, their whole team came after me. Dennis Biodrowski, a former Memphis State teammate, was the first man to hit me. I hit him and got on top of him. By then, the rest of the Chiefs were piling on me. That upset the fans in the south stands, and they started coming over the fence to help me.

These were *my* fans. The south stands of the Denver stadium had adopted me in my rookie year. For all of 1965, they had hung out banners pushing me for Rookie-of-the-Year. They were still bringing the banners, stating sentiments like "We Love The Bull," and "Bull Bramlett For Mayor." This was my cheering section, always at their rowdiest when I was jarring the fillings loose from a guy's teeth. So when I went down under that pile of Chiefs, they emptied the stands.

It took the officials several minutes to convince the fans to leave the field. The game was almost over when my fracas with the Chiefs broke loose, but after the fans got stirred up, it took almost a half hour to play the final three minutes. The officials threw me out of the game, and I never knew why. I guess they thought removing me would calm everyone else down so they could finish the game and go home.

Even without their fanatical loyalty to me, the fans in the south stands had a strong rivalry with the Chiefs. They didn't like it when after every score they made, the Chiefs sent an Indian rider in full headdress out on a horse to circle the field. The Chiefs scored a lot that day, so the fans stayed in an uproar most of the game.

I liked the game of football as well, I think, as anyone who ever played it. I liked the physical contact, the hitting. I never went out just to get through a game; I wanted in on every play. I was there to stop people, but I tried to do it cleanly. Once after I had blind-sided Buffalo tackle Tom Keating at the end of a play, I asked Dick Hudson, Buffalo tackle from Memphis, to apologize for me. I wanted Tom to know that I wasn't the kind who wanted to hurt a man after he was down. When I saw Dick again, I asked if he gave Tom my message.

"Yeah," he answered, "but he told me to save it. He told me to tell you it was his own fault for not knowing better than to go on the same field with you unarmed." Dick grinned and added, "Well, actually, he said he might carry a knife on the field the next time we have to play against you."

It really bothered me to get bad rap for hard hitting. Football is a contact sport. I never took the field without expecting to sacrifice my body. I know everybody hates to lose, but I have never been able to believe that anybody else hates to lose the way I hate to. All my life I wanted to play for a winner, but even as a kid, I never was that fortunate. The Broncos were 0 and 7 in 1966 when rumors about a coaching change began. I came home one day after practice with the big news.

"You won't believe what happened today," I told Nancy. "Sure I will," she said. "I'll bet you have a new coach."

"You already knew about it? How?"

"I didn't hear it officially," she answered, "but there's been so much talk, it can't be a surprise to anyone. Isn't that what happens when you're losing?"

"Yeah," I agreed, "but there's more to the story. Guess who the new coach is." I couldn't keep the grin off my face.

"Well, let's see . . . since you look like a cat that swallowed a mouse, I'm going to guess. Ray Malavasi!"

She knew how much I respected Ray and how indebted I felt to him for giving me a chance to play pro ball in Denver. "You're right. For now, he's the interim head coach," I explained, "but if we can win enough ball games, maybe the job will be permanent."

I thought every member of the team would pull for him, and I was right. Things began coming together for us. Coach Malavasi inspired us to work with each other as a team. We won four of our last seven games, and suddenly we were looking like a good ball club.

Our last home game was against San Diego. It was a crucial game for them, and it was important to me because of what happened in an earlier game. Max Speedie, who was then head coach, had instructed me, "Bull, for four quarters of football, I don't care what is happening anywhere else on the field. Your job is to watch Alworth. If he moves, I want you to get him. If he goes to the bathroom, you go to the bathroom with him. If he bats an eye, you're there in his face. You got it?" Few players could match the grace and speed of Chargers flanker Lance Alworth's moves. Out of the University of Arkansas, he was affectionately called "Bambi," and I knew it would be like matching strides with a deer to contain him for an entire game.

After three quarters of having me all over him, he came up to me and said, "Man, what are you trying to do?" I grinned at him and said, "Wherever you go, I'm going. I'm going with you even if you go to the bathroom. So stay on the field!" He just shook his head and walked away. The Chargers won that game, although "Bambi" had a disappointing day. Denver, however, won the season-ending game with a 20–17 victory, knocking San Diego off the throne in the Western Division.

Late in this last game, the Chargers were leading. They had driven down to our eight yard line. We held them on the third down. They were getting ready to kick a field goal when Ray

Jacobs came over and said, "Bull, when they snap the ball, I'm going to come down on this guard and if you'll come around me, you can slide through the hole and block the field goal." Ray, a tough 285-pound tackle, hit the guard, and I was ready. I slid right around him and never slowed down. When I blocked the field goal attempt, the ball took one bounce and came up into my arms. I took off down the sideline and ran 86 yards for a touchdown. That run set a Broncos' club record which stands today. It was a thrill for me because it put us ahead. Earlier that day, Kansas City had beaten the Jets in New York, so our victory over the Chargers clinched the title in the West for the Chiefs. They went on to play in the First Super Bowl against the Green Bay Packers.

Just when things were going our way, the entire structure was pulled apart. The way it was handled made us wonder if management actually understood what made us click. We were in Buffalo playing our last game of the season when the newspapers carried the story that in 1967 Lou Saban, former Buffalo coach who at that time was out of football, would be our new head coach. Our players were stunned. Our team was improving in every game under Coach Malavasi, and we were looking forward to strengthening our few weak positions with the upcoming draft. I think every one of my teammates would agree today that we believed we were ready to challenge the best in the NFL.

Lou Saban came in, bringing his own coaching staff, and disrupted our entire program. Players who were just coming into their own were scattered around the league in trades—players who became All-Pro Hall-of-Famers on other clubs. What we thought would be our finest hour fizzled into a disappointment for all of us.

I had played all of the 1966 season with an injured shoulder. In that last home game against the Chargers, I received both Denver and American Football League Player-Of-The-Week honors. Our last game was against Miami, and for it I received the Hustle Award. We beat the Dolphins 17-7 that day. I dropped Miami back Joe Auer for a loss of five yards and quarterback Dick Wood for a loss of eleven that took them out of field goal range. I knocked down a Wood pass on a play that eventually forced a missed field goal and teamed with Jerry Hopkins to drop John Stofa, back-up quarterback, for a loss of twelve, then soloed on Stofa for losses of seven and sixteen yards on successive plays.

There is something very special about an honor that comes to you from your peers: you know that they know what you're worth! I knew when I was selected to play in the Pro Bowl that I should not be playing with my injuries, but I would never have missed it.

The Kansas City Chiefs had lost to the Green Bay Packers in the Super Bowl but still placed several players on the Pro Bowl roster. The game was played in Oakland. During practice some of the Chiefs came to me and apologized for the unsportsmanlike play that Coach Stram devised to get me in our game a few weeks earlier. Lenny Dawson said they wanted to take Nancy and me out to dinner to make amends. I had no hard feelings against them, and Nancy and I enjoyed the evening at a Japanese restaurant with them. We thought it was a super gesture from some great guys.

By Pro Bowl game time, it was like a summer monsoon in northern California. Heavy rains had hit the area, and the football field was knee deep in water. I was playing right outside linebacker, positioned next to Buck Buchanan of the Chiefs. As we came up to get set for a play, I noticed something odd about Buck. When I got a chance, I said, "Man, you have lost a shoe. It must be out here somewhere in this mud." He just grinned at me and answered, "Heck, Bull, that happened three plays back. I've done got used to being without it!"

Before the quarter ended, he lost the other one. We couldn't find them in all the mud and water, so Buck played most of that game without shoes. After it was all over, I told him if he had played the Super Bowl game barefoot, Kansas City might have won it. He looked me in the eye and winked. "Yeah, Bull. And if you had played out of your shoes today like I did, we might have won this one."

That game was one for the record book in unpredictability. At halftime, the West was so far ahead (26-0) that the league office made out the game checks to *us*. The winners received $3,000; the losers, $1,500. But in the final outcome, the situation had so reversed itself that we had to wait around while new checks were made. It was one of those wild, slapstick days when anything can happen, but none of that lessened the significance of my being there. The coaches and players select the Pro Bowl candidates; they know who does the job. I appreciated being a part of it.

I returned home to Memphis relieved to have a chance to rest my injured shoulder. But after two weeks of complete rest, it was apparent that I needed surgery. I went over to Campbell Clinic in Memphis for Dr. Marcus Stewart to examine me. The X-rays did not show what was actually wrong. I could not raise my arm; I had to use my right hand to move and manipulate my left. Dr. Stewart operated, unsure of what he would find. In exploratory surgery, he discovered that all the small muscles had drawn down into my back. Never having done similar surgery, he had the operation filmed. The muscles which had been detached and out of use for all those weeks since the injury had deteriorated. Some of them had to be tied off. Where possible, Dr. Stewart pulled up the small muscles with prongs and fastened them back to the large muscle. It was tedious surgery requiring seven hours.

During my stay in the hospital, Nancy attempted to reassure me. "I know what you're thinking," she told me, "but don't worry, you'll play again. You're too tough for this to get you. You'll be back, maybe better than ever."

"Hadn't even thought about it," I insisted. I fixed her with my I-don't-want-to-hear-this look. "Forget it," I said, and went back to sleep. But I had thought about it. In fact, I had thought of little else since I woke up and learned the extent of the damage to my shoulder.

I recovered well, but my reach on that side decreased by two inches. In order for the muscle to grow back and heal, I had to wear a brace to keep it immobile for eight weeks. After the brace came off, I spent the rest of the off-season building up strength on that side. My shoulder never came back to full strength, nor could I ever abuse it without developing a constant, nagging pain, but because I was so determined to play, I went out and threw myself into the game for five more years. Pain was something I had learned to live with.

When other players let up because of injuries, I sometimes upset them with my cruel sense of humor. One day after hearing several complain, I wrapped myself all the way up and down with bandages and tape, and went out to practice. I looked like a mummy.

"Don't tell Bull you're hurting," my teammates told each other. "You'll get no sympathy from him. He doesn't know the meaning of the word."

I think one of the reasons coaches and players alike always respected Joe Namath was that he ignored pain and went on giving all he had to the game. With his bad knees, you might think you didn't have to worry about him, but that is just when he would hurt you. He could skip back a few steps on those bad knees faster than most quarterbacks who were not hurting, then set up and fire the ball instantaneously.

During my first season with Denver I was able to blast in and sack him a few times, but I never really got to know Joe the man that year.

After meeting him in Memphis at the Pro-Am golf tournament, I looked forward to seeing him again. In our first game with the Jets in Denver in 1966, Joe and Ray Abruzzi, defensive back for the Jets, came out to our house for dinner. Ray had been a buddy of Joe's since their college days at the University of Alabama. The night they came, Nancy made good her promise to Joe to cook fried chicken, hot biscuits, and gravy. She made some kind of dish out of green beans, mushrooms, and onion rings that Joe couldn't stop eating. After that, she added it to the menu when she knew he was coming. Nancy liked Joe, and the boys were crazy about him too. It was fun for the whole family when he came.

I remember one particular Sunday afternoon game with the Jets at Mile High Stadium. Joe had eaten at our apartment the evening before. It was a tough game; any game with Namath quarterbacking was going to be tough. He could be one of the most relaxed guys you ever saw in your home, cracking jokes, laughing with your kids, but on the field after the kickoff, it was all business.

He could back-pedal, set up, and get a pass off so quick that it was almost impossible to keep him from scoring on you. I got to him four times that Sunday and really hit him. It seemed that every time I got him, we would both end up lying on the ground looking toward the end zone just in time to see the ref signal a touchdown. No matter how fast I fired in there, he could get the ball off a split second before I reached him.

Joe never got upset with a man for a hard, clean, head-on tackle. The best quarterbacks all expect to be hit, and I consider Joe Namath the best to ever play the game.

After we played the Jets that game, a feature came out in *Sports Illustrated* about Joe. I took a lot of ribbing about the way I treated my friends after that issue was released. In the story Joe explained to the reporter that we were really good friends. He said, "Bramlett is such a good friend, he will invite you out to his house to dinner on Saturday night, then the next day, he will go out on the football field and try to knock it all out of you."

13

Mile High to Sea Level

The July 18, 1967 *Denver Post* ran a story stating that "Bull Bramlett left town Monday night to return to his home in Memphis. There are reports that he is demanding a four-year no-cut contract. 'This is not true,' says Bramlett; 'I was only asking for two, and they wouldn't even quote me a figure. I just wish they would trade me or give me my release—or something.'"

The Commercial Appeal in Memphis ran the story with added details:

Lou Saban, Denver's new general manager and head coach, said, "The negotiations are at a complete stalemate. At this moment we are too far apart to think about getting together." He also says that the Denver point of concern is Bramlett's injured shoulder which required an operation after last season. When asked about the shoulder, Bramlett replied, "It's not my shoulder they are worried about. They just don't want to pay me what I'm worth. They know my shoulder is good. They haven't mentioned my shoulder to me. My doctor, one of the country's top orthopedic surgeons, says I am completely recovered and ready to play. I have been lifting weights, bench-pressed 300 pounds, and hit the blocking sled at Memphis State without any pain." Bramlett added that he would not back down from what he felt he deserved on the basis of his two previous years with Denver. He said he had not talked directly with Saban. Bramlett made clear that he was not seeking "a whole lot of money but I am asking for some security." He also made clear that he had not been given an opportunity to talk to Saban. According to Bramlett, "Lou Saban doesn't have anything to do with the players. He tells everybody in camp that he has a 10-year no-cut contract and he is going to be here but he doesn't know about anybody else."

On July 26, another headline from the Memphis *Press-Scimitar* carried this news: "Dolphin Coach Is Happy About Bramlett Trade." The Dolphins gave up their following year's top draft choice to bring me to Miami. They were a new expansion team in their second year, looking for all the help they could get. They had drafted and signed Bob Griese out of Purdue. "We have signed some people who can improve our club," said Miami Coach George Wilson. "We have filled in a gap with Bull Bramlett as an outside linebacker to go with Frank Emanuel." Frank was a middle linebacker out of the University of Tennessee.

My shoulder's condition at the end of the '66 season had probably made it difficult for the Bronco club to believe that I could continue to play. I packed my gear and swapped Mile High stadium for the seashore.

In Florida I quickly found enough "birds of a feather" to keep my usual pace of drinking, fighting, and staying out at night. Frank Emanuel and I ran with Wahoo McDaniel, a big linebacker out of Oklahoma who came to Miami from New York. Wahoo was a wrestler. In New York he was so well known for his wrestling that when we played ball there, the fans never let him forget it. During the game, if Wahoo made a tackle, the announcer would bleat out over the loudspeaker, "Tackle made by—guess-s who-oo!" The people in the stands answered by cupping their hands around their mouths and yelling back, "Wa-hoo-oo!"

Before regular season play began, we played an exhibition game in Memphis against the Buffalo Bills. Whit Canale, a fellow Memphian and University of Tennessee defensive end, played in that game. Frank Emanuel, Whit, and I all had a good game defensively in spite of my accidental hit on teammate Abner Haynes on a punt return. Apparently, one of us zigged when a zag would have been wiser. I knocked him out and had to help him off the field. But he was soon back in the game, which we won 10-7.

Stan Mitchell, a Tennessee fullback, was a Miami rookie that year. On his first road trip we were assigned to the same room. He told me later on that his first night on the road was almost his last. He was in our room on the eighth floor waiting for me to come in. It got very late; I was never in early. Stan said he was lying in bed half asleep when he heard someone running hard down the hall. He jumped up just as I got my key in the lock and burst into the room.

It wasn't the right time for long explanations. I had blood all over my face and hands, so I headed for the bathroom, yelling at him, "Get over to the window and see what's going on outside! Do you see any cops?" I got a glimpse of Stan's face as I ran into the bathroom; his eyes were as big as saucers.

When I came out, he was peering out from behind the draperies. "What do you see?" I asked.

"Two police cars with red lights flashing. But I don't see anybody in them."

"No," I said, "they're in here looking for me. Turn out the lights and get in bed."

We heard voices in the hall for awhile, but no one came to our door. I knew Stan was thinking he had some kind of outlaw, maybe a murderer, to room with, so I told him not to worry; I had beat up some guys in a joint, and they had called the cops on me.

Stan and I became road trip roommates, but after that first night with me, he wouldn't accept my invitations to go out. On one trip, we were in New York to play the Jets, and I was going out with some other players on Saturday night.

When we got in the hotel elevator to go down, a big Spanish-looking dude was already in it. He heard us talking about the game the next day, and just as he stepped out into the lobby, he looked at us and said, "I guess you bozos know the Jets are going to kick your rears."

The nasty look on his face and his tone of voice got to me. I did the lowest, meanest thing I could think of—I walked up to within two inches of him and spit in his face. He pulled a knife on me and I went for him. He jumped backward toward the elevator, but before he could reach it, I had my coat off and wrapped around my arm. I told him I was going to take the knife and use it on him. He got inside the elevator, but because it was one of those old types with a wire cage, I was able to get a foot inside it so it wouldn't close. Then I shoved the door open and hit him before he could get to me with his knife. By then I was furious. When Carl Noonan, one of my teammates, got to us, I was straddling the guy, pounding his head against the floor. If I hadn't been stopped, I might have killed him.

Noonan told Stan about the incident, but Stan never said a word about it to me. I knew he wanted to stay out of trouble, and I respected that. But I think he decided on another night that staying in the room didn't always insure his safety, at least not when I was around.

We were in Buffalo, and I was out drinking until late. As I went to our room, I could see a big wedding reception going full-blast in a suite at the end of the hall. I was tired and when I got in my room, I took off my pants and shirt and flopped down on the bed. I was already half asleep when the noise down the hall finally got to me.

"Stan, are you awake?"

He said, "I know what you mean. They're sure having a good time down there."

I bounced up. "They're not going to be having a good time after I get there." In nothing but a pair of boxer shorts, I took off down the hall.

The door to the suite was open. The rooms were filled with people milling about in tuxes and long gowns. The bride looked so shocked when I ran in that I tried to be nice. I said, "You people are too noisy . . ." Before I could finish, somebody made an off-color remark to me, and that did it! I started yelling.

"My roommate and I have put up with all of this we are going to. We've got an important ball game to play tomorrow, and we can't sleep for your noise. This is gonna' stop right now. You hear me?"

When I started yelling, they all froze. While I had their attention, I added, "I'm going back down to my room, and if I hear one more peep out of you, I'm coming back down here and whip every last one of you—and that goes for you women too!" I stomped out and slammed the door behind me.

Stan and I didn't hear another sound all night. I don't know how those people got out of there so quietly.

❏   ❏   ❏

I was constantly telling Stan how you have to stay ready for anything. He seemed to see me as the "old pro," so I gave him advice on how to stay psyched up for the game. "Stan," I said, "this game is 90 percent mental."

"Bull, you're full of bull! Are you trying to tell me you got that bandaged leg and taped hand working crossword puzzles? Looks pretty physical to me."

"Naw. I'm just telling you, you gotta' ignore pain."

Stan squinted his big brown eyes at me and argued, "That's not too easy when your stitches are still tender." Stan was just recovering from an appendectomy.

"Then you talk to it. I just keep saying to my shoulder or knee, 'You're not hurt, you don't hurt, you're okay.' You can't let every little thing get to you. Take a positive approach to pain just like you do to the game."

"Like when you know you're going to get tromped, you just say this isn't happening?"

"You've got it all wrong," I told him. "You don't *ever* know you are going to get tromped. You've got to put yourself into an unbeatable frame of mind. You don't consider the possibility of losing. You think only of winning!"

It was my personal theory that what happened on a particular play came out of what was already in your head. For instance, lots of players complain about the conditions of the field, that it is uneven or soft. Instead, I tell myself, "The condition of the field means nothing; I can play just as well and win in a cow pasture, or down at the old Triangle in Memphis where I used to play when I was a kid."

In the pros, you assume that everybody there has the physical ability to play the game. So I figured the difference had to be mental. I think most of the guys agreed but would never admit it to me.

"Yeah, Bull," they'd laugh, "it works just like telling a guy who gets hit by a train that it's all in his mind."

Not long after I moved to Miami, Norm Evans invited me to chapel services. Norm had played with the Houston Oilers, coming to Miami in their first year as an expansion team in 1966. In Houston, Johnny Baker, who was one of his teammates, had initiated a chapel service before each home game. Johnny invited his pastor to speak to the players and coaches, and Norm liked the idea. After coming to Miami, he wanted to continue it to encourage the Dolphins to become involved in Christian activities. He had not been able to stir up much interest among the other players, but he felt that it would catch on if he could get it started.

"Doc" Eshleman, who had founded Bibletown in Boca Raton, encouraged him and promised to help. "Doc" was a minister who had given up a big church in Detroit to move to Florida to open up a Christian center where people from all over the country could gather for study and worship.

When Norm told me about his dream for the program, he said it was something that he and his wife, Bobbie, had been praying for, and he thought it would make us better ball players. "Bull," he asked me, "don't you think the Christians on the team ought to have an opportunity to worship together?"

I liked Norm, I had gone to church regularly as a kid, so I said, "Sure, why not?"

That first Sunday morning chapel service was a big disappointment to Norm and "Doc." Only two or three Dolphins showed up. I bellowed out those old hymns as loudly as I could, hoping some of the other players would hear and join us, but without effect. *Okay,* I said to myself, *so we'll have to do this another way.* To Norm, I said, "Don't worry about it. They'll be here next Sunday. You'll see."

On the following Sunday morning, even before chapel time, the room was packed with Dolphins. Norm was happy—and if any of the players against whose lives I had made personal threats were unhappy, they were careful to hide it.

I respected Norm and "Doc" enough to put up a good front

for chapel service. I even participated. I still remembered those two Bible verses I had memorized as a kid, so one Sunday I would quote Hebrews 5:8, the next Sunday, Hebrews 5:9.

A young expansion team cannot expect great success against experienced, veteran teams, but toward the end of the season, we were beginning to gel. The San Diego Chargers came into the Orange Bowl in December all fired up to beat us for the second time. In a great effort by our entire team, we beat them 41-24. Bob Griese cinched his starting quarterback position by connecting on 15 of 28 passes for 145 yards.

I had two interceptions, seven tackles, and three assists. After the game, Linebacker Coach Bob Pellegrini walked up to me and said, "I want to shake the hand of the best 105-pound linebacker in the American Football League."

"You don't mean that," I corrected him. "Not unless I have lost a hundred pounds in this game."

"Okay, make that 205 pounds," he agreed. "Whatever you say. And not just the lightweight of the American League. I'll throw in the National League, too."

Pellegrini could be counted on to let his boys know when he was pleased with them. We had just set an expansion team record high over the "old pros," and I earned his praise by returning one of my two interceptions twenty-two yards to the San Diego five, setting up our final touchdown.

It was one of those peaches-and-roses games that persuades you that you have turned the corner. I didn't even flinch when the coach gripped my hand. I had been playing for weeks with my right thumb so badly torn up that the trainers had to perform a lengthy treatment before each game. The thumb flopped around like a chicken with its neck broken, so they taped it tightly to my hand, shot it full of novacaine, then taped over it heavily. That routine got me through the season, until I could get back to Memphis and check into Campbell Clinic for the usual off-season repairs. While fixing my thumb for the following spring, a muscle was removed from my arm to transplant to the thumb so it would have adequate movement.

I played with injuries so much that I would kid my teammates during calisthenics by howling and letting out pained yells until no one else dared complain. The pain was real. I did a lot of other crazy things to relieve the boredom of routine. Sometimes I'd show up at practice in a Halloween mask; when leaving the practice field, I'd baseball slide into the sideline. Naturally, I gestured myself safe, which was always good for a laugh.

I took everything to the extreme. I pushed people to the very edge. I was unmanageable, with a temper that I had never even tried to control. I was so determined to get my own way that I now find it surprising that I had any friends. I guess the ones who liked me thought they ought to hang around just to see what I would do next.

At the end of the 1967 season when the ballots were cast to elect Pro Bowl players, I was selected to play for the defense. It was my second consecutive Pro Bowl. I had played with the West the previous year as a Bronco, and now I would be on the side of the East. But instead of feeling good about where I was in my career, I felt only a vindictive sense of pride. I had never outgrown the compulsive feeling of having to prove my own worth to others. My first thought was that this would prove to Lou Saban and the Denver management that they had made a mistake in letting me go. I clung to my resentment as if it were a trophy I had awarded myself. I wish I could have seen how little such things matter.

Nancy laid it out for me when she said, "John, you say you don't care what anyone thinks, then you worry because they're not thinking what you think they should. You know what I think *they* think? They just think about winning. They don't care where you play ball or how well you play. Where you are today is the least of their worries." I am sure she was right, but at the time, I wouldn't admit it. When others rubbed me the wrong way, I wanted to make them pay somehow, even if it was just in my own mind.

I missed much of the pleasure I could have enjoyed in the high points of my career because of my own excesses. One of the big problems with my capacity to enjoy any success was that I couldn't have fun unless I was drinking. This is just one of the lies all drunks tell themselves to excuse their behavior. Though the alcoholic may not actually voice his excuse for drinking, somewhere within himself, he feels compelled to manufacture an explanation. I would never have admitted it, but I knew I fell short of a standard I believed I had to keep, so I looked for a way to justify my actions. I had it worked out to a fine art. The habits I could not justify to myself, I just blamed on someone else.

The trip to Jacksonville, Florida, for the Pro Bowl couldn't have been much fun for Nancy; when I wasn't practicing football, I was drinking.

My teammates elected me Special Teams Captain for the game. We won over the West by a narrow margin when George Blanda shanked a field goal attempt for the West that went wide, but winning in a Pro Bowl matchup was not as important as playing ball with the very best, rubbing shoulders with men I admired as football's finest. I look back on those post-season games as high points in my career.

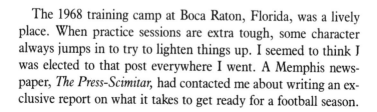

The 1968 training camp at Boca Raton, Florida, was a lively place. When practice sessions are extra tough, some character always jumps in to try to lighten things up. I seemed to think I was elected to that post everywhere I went. A Memphis newspaper, *The Press-Scimitar*, had contacted me about writing an exclusive report on what it takes to get ready for a football season.

What went on some of the time, however, the *Press-Scimitar* couldn't have printed.

Every team has its annual rookie show. I had charge of ours, so naturally it was a howling success. I set up a portable toilet and put a rookie in it smoking a big cigar. Every time things got quiet, he was supposed to open the door and tell a joke on one of the coaches. After awhile, we noticed he wasn't opening the door on cue, so I checked on him. He had gotten so sick on cigar smoke, he had passed out. He forgot to tell me that he had never even smoked a cigarette before.

Two of the rookies, running backs Jim Kiick and Larry Csonka ("Zonk") arrived too late to rehearse for the rookie show, but we found them enthusiastic about everything except curfew. We suspected from the first that they had hidden talents, so we took them out drinking two nights in a row. The first night, we took them around to all the joints so they would know where to go when we weren't with them. The next night, Zonk dived off a bridge onto a sandy beach about twenty feet below. He kept telling linebacker Wahoo, defensive end Mel Branch, defensive tackle Ray Jacobs, and me what a good diver he was, and we decided he should demonstrate the art for us. We stopped the car on a bridge and let Zonk out. Unfortunately, there was no water below. When he hit the beach, it knocked him out. Had he not been so drunk, it probably would have killed him.

We occasionally stayed in the dorm and entertained ourselves quietly, or at least less uproariously. Bob Neff and Mel played the guitar. Charlie Fowler played banjo. Center Tom Goode sang country songs. I cracked them up with my church songs and sermons. I'd stand there and tell all those guys that they were on their way to Hell.

Quarterback Bob Griese and flanker Jack Clancy had a constant chess game going. Wahoo rounded up everyone with money for his poker games. Billy Neighbors, offensive guard, was our financial adviser. He was a stockbroker in the off-season and was the Miami Dolphins' "clubhouse lawyer." He had all the answers!

Asking rookies to sing their college fight songs was standard procedure in camp. Dick Anderson, a defensive back from Colorado, refused, so we dragged him out of the dining hall and threw him into a lake, fully dressed. The next night, before he was asked, he stood up and started bellowing out his song. We knew then we were in trouble if he couldn't play ball better than he could sing.

Nancy and I lived upstairs in the Villa Apartments in Miami. Jim Kiick and his wife, Alice, took an apartment on the ground floor beneath ours. We called them "the kids" so much that even Andy and Don, who were now seven and six, often asked if "the kids" were coming to dinner. Nancy usually cooked enough for them to eat with us because we enjoyed having them around. I kept telling Jim I was going to start claiming them on my income tax.

After dinner, Jim and I could pull the fastest disappearing act in history. My favorite bar, One South, was close to home, so we usually started drinking there. As the evening progressed, I liked to move on, looking for action. Jim and Alice had not been married long, so he sometimes chickened out on me, probably at Alice's insistence. I went anyway.

For a time earlier in our marriage, Nancy tried to fit into my lifestyle. It's easy to see now that she was only trying to create the kind of companionship between us that she was convinced a marriage ought to have. She tried to learn to smoke and drink, but she gave up on both after a night that almost deprived my boys of a mother—a night that should have made me realize that something was seriously wrong in my life.

I had taken Nancy to one of the joints where I liked to hang out. A woman I knew came up and openly asked me to call her up and come over to see her, ignoring Nancy, who heard the whole thing. I'm sure Nancy suspected that a lot went on that I didn't tell her, but no one had ever been that brazen about it. She couldn't handle it.

On our way home, she didn't say anything, but suddenly she reached for the car door handle. I was able to react quickly enough to grab her arm as the door swung open. I was able somehow to hold on and keep her from jumping.

I can still see the pain and hopelessness in her eyes that told me she had reached the breaking point. I must have realized that night something of the love she had for me, because in a strange way there was a stronger bond between us after that. I didn't change my lifestyle, but I tried to protect Nancy from feeling so embarrassed about what I did. I felt so strongly about it that I worked a guy over for telling a "Bramlett story" at a party.

"The next time you want to tell your wife something," I hissed, "first, you tell her what *you* did! Then maybe she won't even be listening by the time you get around to telling what 'Bramlett' did. When I want my wife to know something, *I'll* tell her. You got that?" He got it.

One night at One South someone came in and told Frank Emanuel, Manny Fernandez, Jim Kiick, and me that it was raining. Frank and I decided to go out and splash around in the puddles in the parking lot. After getting wet, we thought we might as well go for a swim, so we went across to the park and dived into a canal. We started swimming around and yelling. Jim thought we were drowning. He knew I wasn't a good swimmer, so he came lumbering down the hill and jumped in to rescue me. While he was trying to get me out, we both went under a few times. Every time Jim got his head above water, he yelled for Frank to help him. Frank had found a bunch of ducks and was paddling after them. He just stayed with the ducks.

When Jim got me out, we were covered with slime and seaweed. Suddenly I realized I didn't have my denture plate. I raised so much cain that someone called the cops. As we were not far from our apartment, they told us to go home.

I found my denture plate in the bathroom the next morning. I hadn't even had it with me the evening before.

We had games in California on two consecutive Sundays, so the team flew to San Diego for the first game, then stayed over in Palo Alto the following week to play Oakland. We were free to go out sightseeing Sunday night and Monday, but none of us had any wheels. I noticed some golf carts parked over near the hotel golf course, so I got one and took off, making the rounds of all the joints downtown. When I came back, I just pulled the cart up to my hotel and parked at the door. The next morning I went out, got in my golf cart, and drove out on the freeway.

All that day I drove around the city, stopping in places that looked interesting. When I met people needing transportation, I gave them a lift. It was a fun day, soaking up California sun and other amenities.

The next morning in the hotel coffee shop I found George Wilson holding a newspaper, with my Dolphin blazer across his lap. I wasn't about to claim the jacket because I couldn't remember where I had left it. Then I caught a glimpse of a headline in the paper, *"The Phantom Golf Cart Driver—Have You Seen This Man?"* The picture under it was of a man breezing down a busy expressway in a golf cart. It looked very familiar. Ignoring it, I ordered a cup of coffee.

George held up the jacket, but before he could speak I said, "Hey, Coach, you found my jacket, didn't you? Don't you remember, someone stole it from me right after we got off the plane?"

He looked at me for a minute before answering. "To answer your questions, no, I didn't find it, the police did. And no, I don't remember your coat being stolen."

I thanked him for the coat and dropped the subject. So did George.

Another of my career pictures was even less flattering than the Expressway Phantom, though more profitable for the photographer. Jay Spencer, a news photographer, wanted a picture to enter in a national contest and asked me to be his subject. I didn't mind, so during a home game, I posed on the sideline for him. I leaned back on the bench in a relaxed manner, with a cigar dangling from my lips. He seemed pleased with the results and posted his entry. During the off-season, Spencer called me up to tell me he was sending me a box of cigars. His photo of me lolling on the Dolphin bench had won first place in the national contest, plus a considerable cash prize.

We had some fine, young players coming in as we approached

the 1969 season, and our rookies of the year before had ended their first season playing like seasoned veterans. But just as I was feeling good about our team becoming a winner, I learned that I was being traded.

14

Beantown

When Joe Namath and the "Super Jets" won Super Bowl Three over Baltimore in 1969, Clive Rush, as offensive coordinator for New York, masterminded the victory. Soon afterward, the lure of a head coaching position moved him to Boston. I was in Memphis when I had my first talk with him after learning that the Patriots had traded Nick Buoniconti to Miami for me. I felt good about Coach Rush wanting me enough to be willing to part with Buoniconti, a great middle linebacker.

Coach Rush was complimentary and enthusiastic over the phone. He said, "Bramlett, you're going to give us what we need on the outside. I've watched you; you are a fierce competitor and that's exactly what we're looking for. And I wanted you because you know as much about defense as any man who plays the game."

"Well, I know defense is more than just defending a goal post," I answered, not quite sure how to handle his praise.

"That's what I mean, Bramlett, I know all about you. I know you are a team man. Oh, I've heard a few stories, but they don't concern me. You know, if you go all out on anything, some people are going to say you're too aggressive. You just take that aggression out on the field and we'll get along fine."

I was never at ease with compliments. When they were not expressed in my presence, I could enjoy them; I just never learned to accept them personally without feeling awkward. I had been told all my life that you can't let what people say become too important, even though I felt a deep inner need for approval. But somehow after all my efforts to gain it, it never brought quite the satisfaction I expected. Praise seemed to trigger memories from the past that I preferred to keep buried.

When my dad died, Nancy and I flew home for his funeral. Looking at him, I had a strange feeling that he had taken with him something that belonged to me, something I needed.

I remembered all those years when a little kid would have given his life just to have heard him say, "Son, I am proud of you, and I love you." It never happened. I stood alone by my dad's casket for a long time, thinking how cold and forbidding he looked. Nothing had changed.

After that, my own attitude toward my boys changed a little. I had always been proud of my sons, but everything I had ever done with them was aimed at teaching them to be tough. I began to ease up on that, making my roughhousing with them more affectionate. I didn't want Andy or Don to ever feel that I held back something that belonged to them.

After moving my family to Boston in 1969, I went immediately to training camp. Nancy was busy getting the boys settled in school and was looking forward to acquainting herself with the city. She hardly got settled before she was making plans for us to visit all the famous landmarks. I came in one night and found her sitting in the floor, surrounded by maps and brochures.

"Look," she said, pointing out a place on a map. "This is Old North Church. You've heard of that."

"Naw," I said, "can't say I have."

She went right on. "Here is Old South Meetinghouse. And the seventeenth century house where Paul Revere lived. Ah, look at this—I want the boys to see Boston Light, the oldest lighthouse in the entire United States. Let's take them there first!"

Uh oh. This was not the Boston I planned to explore. "Nancy, that's nice," I said, "really nice. You take your little boys and go to all your little old 'Meetinghouses' and lighthouses. I think you ought to see all of that historical stuff. But I won't have time. Y'all just go ahead without me."

She did it all. She was constantly telling me what a beautiful old city Boston was. The beauty I saw was its bright lights and the football field at Boston College Stadium where we played our games. During my second year with the Patriots, we played at Harvard. Nancy knew where my interests lay; she knew what to expect of me. Apparently she had come to terms with the way I lived because she didn't cross me. As long as she didn't get in the way of what I wanted to do, I was fairly predictable around the house. I was at home occasionally, playing around with the boys, so I probably appeared to outsiders to be a normal, caring husband and father. I recognized even then that when things were going well it was because Nancy was exercising a lot of diplomacy. The way I looked at it, that was what she was supposed to do.

After ten years, our life together had not changed greatly from its beginning. I still called all the shots. If I had looked deeper than the instant gratification I believed to be my right, I might have developed a more unbiased view of a wife's rights, or at least have admitted that she had some. But I grew up in an atmosphere where there was little room for compassion or arbitration. We had one source of authority, and everyone answered to him, my father. He ruled with an iron fist. No excuses, no second chances, no mercy.

After all those years, I hated that attitude so much that I intended to be different. But I failed to recognize the impossibility of total self-reformation. So I guess I shouldn't be surprised that the nature I hated and would not have consciously chosen, took me over and grew worse.

Soon after I moved to Boston, the newspapers began playing up my reputation as a hustling, hard hitter with a fitting nickname. Everywhere I went I was "The Bull." All the papers carried the story of how I got the name, but they got their information from my teammates, so the account of my running through the fence during a baseball game took on some added color. As a joke, I finally roped off an area and hung up a sign designating it "Bull's Lounge" so the reporters would know where to find me.

In my opinion, football produces a closer camaraderie than any other sport. The rough nature of the game squeezes players into a momentary dependency upon each other in which no one succeeds unless everyone does his job. I had some good friends on the Patriots' team; some I still stay in touch with.

Mike Taliaferro came over to the Patriots with Clive Rush when he became head coach. Mike, who had been backup quarterback to Joe Namath in New York, became our first-string quarterback. He was good, in fact, he was far better than our game results indicated. We were shy of the strength we needed up front, and it is hard to throw from a prone position. Mike must have been making up for his frustrations on the field when he thought up ways to kid rookie ball players.

I can't claim total innocence here. I always chose the victim, usually one that we agreed needed a lesson in humility. After we selected our rookie for the dubious honor, Mike would call him up and establish himself as Joe Smith, sports reporter for *The Boston Globe*. He then told the rookie he had talked with the coach about who was the most promising rookie in camp.

At that point, our rookie became excited and talkative. Mike taped the entire telephone "interview," with questions and answers designed to embarrass the loose-tongued rookie whenever, inevitably, the whole team heard the tape. Mike always ended the telephone conversation with a request for a photograph "to include with the article in Sunday's paper." None ever refused to have his picture taken, though the circumstances made it ridiculous.

Training camp consisted of exhausting workouts combined with many hours of classroom work, all in very casual attire. A typical afternoon workout began around one-thirty in the vicinity of the locker room. Knowing that all the other players would be present in cut off shorts and tee shirts, Mike would have our superstar rookie scheduled to come dressed for his photo session in a suit and tie. The resulting hilarity when the rookie realized that no photographer was going to show up worked wonders in deflating a conceited rookie's ego. Besides that, our craziness brought some comic relief when the tensions of training camp got to us.

Joe Namath opened a private club in New York with a couple of other guys, and when it succeeded they opened a new *Bachelors Three* in Boston. I was invited to the grand opening. I knew it was going to be one of those elegant dress affairs, so I had an idea that I thought would help loosen it up a bit. After football practice, I put on some old sweats and tennis shoes, turned a baseball cap backwards on my head, and took my partial plate out of my mouth.

At *Bachelors Three*, I stood grinning toothlessly at the doorman and asked, "Is that there Joe Namath here?" The fancy-dressed doorkeeper wasn't about to let me in. I insisted, "You go tell that Joe Namath that one of his good buddies is here to see him." When he relayed my message, Namath laughed so hard he couldn't speak at first. He finally motioned for the doorman to let me in. "Go let that crazy thing in here," he said, "I know him." Nothing I did seemed to surprise Joe.

He came out to our house on Don's birthday. Nancy had all the birthday trappings—hats and balloons, and a big birthday cake. Joe and I clowned around with Andy and Don while Nancy had fun getting it all on film with her movie camera.

I was the clown prince with my drinking buddies and my teammates. Away from them, I was uptight, high-strung, ticking away, read to explode. Nancy could take bad situations and find a way to pull something good out of them for the boys. I usually found a way to mess up every special occasion.

I spoiled every Christmas for them with my drinking and fighting, many times ending up in jail. Getting drunk was so common to me that when Christmas came, I thought I had to do more of it, or I wasn't really celebrating. Drunk or sober, it never took much provocation to start me fighting. Every Christmas Eve, before the night ended, Nancy was out trying to locate me and get me home so I would stay out of trouble. She covered up as well as she could, but Andy and Don knew what went on. They felt all the fear and uncertainty of wondering what would happen next. After the ugly commotions I caused were over, I would really put on my "Mr. Wonderful" act, promising the moon but delivering nothing.

My tendency to ignore advice almost cost me my life one night in the skies between New Orleans and Boston. We were returning after a game with the Saints, and as usual, I was banged up and hurting. The team doctor had given me an envelope of codeine pills, with instructions to take one every four hours. I swallowed the whole package of pills, then drank one beer after another for as long as I could stay awake. When the plane landed in Boston, my teammates tried to awaken me. Unable to rouse me, they called an ambulance and rushed me to the hospital.

After my stomach was pumped clean, I rallied enough to be able to go home. Jim Cheyunski, a teammate, told me later how fortunate I was that the plane landed when it did. Ten minutes more, the doctors said, would have been fatal for me. I can now see that there were many times when divine intervention was the only thing standing between me and the consequences of my rash behavior.

"Chi" and I, both small for defensive players, became friends soon after I arrived in Boston. One day he told me, "'Bull,' it's a good thing the Pats traded for you because you were on my list when you were playing for Miami."

"Why?" I asked.

"Chi" said, "You blind-sided me and broke two of my ribs. I was covering a punt for Boston and just before I made the tackle, you came in on me like a Mack truck. I was just a rookie then, but I knew enough to catch your number and wait my chance to get even." He laughed and added, "After we got you, I figured we needed you too much to hurt you." "Chi" was good to me. When we were out on strike for several weeks, he and his wife, Pat, invited me to stay in their home.

My second year in Boston was a good year for me, although I was playing hurt most of the time. I had a painful bursa on my elbow from the third week on, and had a torn-up knee that gave me trouble after every game. I knew I was doing my job, and I was receiving substantial coverage in the newspapers as a result.

There was one writeup I appreciated so much that I saved it. Whenever my respected peers had something to say about football, I listened, and this particular column expressed the views of one of the players I respected most, Marty Schottenheimer, who

was then linebacker for the Patriots. Marty's praise made playing
with multiple injuries less painful. The article below appeared in
The Boston Globe.

Excerpts from *Pro Football Weekly*'s article titled "AFC's Best
Outside Linebacker! Bramlett Is The Patriots' Real Star:"

If the Patriots' John "Bull" Bramlett doesn't get all-league honors it will be tantamount to another Brink's robbery. This is the
well-thought-out opinion of Marty Schottenheimer. Despite being
hampered by injuries since pre-season time, "Bull" has been the
club's most consistent performer.

Schottenheimer, who makes a study of the workings of the game
of pro football and those who play it, has a fantastic admiration for
Bramlett and his way of playing football.

"He is the best outside linebacker in the American Conference,
probably the best in all pro football . . . John Bramlett is to outside
linebacking what Dick Butkus is to middle linebacking," Marty
says in praise of his Boston teammate.

Schottenheimer isn't yanking his own chain when he reasons,
"There just isn't a better outside linebacker around . . . you go
down the whole list of them, and you'll find that John Bramlett
should be at the top of the listing."

He has been playing on a severely painful foot injury since the
exhibition season. Knee and arm damage have not helped his physical well-being. Schottenheimer sluffs off the injury aspect. "Forget about them . . . once he gets into the game he is okay, and it
would be impossible for him to play any better than he's playing
right now, so the injury part isn't that important," he says.

Bramlett took some bad-mouthing from Buffalo's O. J. Simpson
in his recently published "novel." It branded "Bull" as a cheap-
shot artist.

Marty explained, "That is stupid. John is not a cheap-shot artist.
He is cut from the same piece of cloth as Dick Butkus, and that is to
do your job to the limit . . . if a ball-carrier is moving a muscle,
make sure he doesn't gain anything by it." Schottenheimer is a
close personal friend of the Bear middle linebacker, Butkus. "I
work out with him, study films with him, and condition with him;
believe me, there is no real difference between Butkus and
Bramlett other than a little size," he declares.

Why then hasn't Bramlett been an AFL all-star?

"That's easy, he's never received the recognition he deserves,"
Marty says. "I have played with those guys who've got recognition," Marty says in a very demanding tone, "and none of 'em
could hold "Bull" Bramlett's dirty socks."

Two games before the season ended, Coach Rush was fired, and John Mazur came to fill the position of head coach for the Patriots. At the end of the season, I was named the *Most Valuable Player* on the squad by my teammates.

"I think you are a great choice for this honor, Bramlett," Coach Mazur said, congratulating me.

I agreed that it was a great honor. "Being selected by my teammates means a lot because they're the ones who know who is doing the job. A part of the reason I work hard is to gain their admiration."

"Well," he said, "you got their votes. No one came near you on the ballots."

"Shoot, Coach, I just love this game. If I had my way I'd play it twelve months a year."

Trainer Bill Bates couldn't let that pass. "Bull, you couldn't live out that wish. Right now, your body is a total wreck. Let's see, you've got a bad elbow, neck, foot, hand, thumb, shoulder, and knee—and that's just on one side!"

"You sound like my wife," I joked. "She keeps more ice packs than she does food stored in the refrigerator."

I took a lot of good-natured kidding about the stuff the newspapers ran. The sports section of *The Boston Globe* carried a drawing of players in action superimposed over each other, all wearing my number 57 on their jerseys. The caption over it read, "The Brave Bull." It was hilarious to hear my buddies express their views of that.

I might have joked convincingly about it, and I certainly did everything I could to create an image of indifference to what others thought, but deep down, more than I wanted anything else, I wanted approval. At last, I had it. I could go back to Memphis riding high. I had some injuries that needed attention, but Campbell Clinic would take care of those. Like my friend Marty said, *forget about them.*

15

When the Walls Fall Down

I opened my eyes and lay still, trying to focus on my surround-ings. In the dim light, I could make out the high bedside table and a single chair. I tensed my muscles to move and felt a sudden sharp pain. Then I remembered; I was in the hospital following an appendectomy. It could not have come at a worse time. I had already done off-season time in Campbell Clinic for knee and el-bow operations in preparation for the 1971 football season. Two weeks before training camp was to open, this appendix trouble flared up, putting me back in the hospital.

I lay awake, listening to the muffled sounds on the busy floor, and thought about how this operation so near the season's open-ing might affect me. I'd just have to ease up a little at first, that's all. I could handle it. I must have dozed off because suddenly I was a little kid being smashed in the face by a big guy with hard eyes and bony knuckles. One of his feet on mine held me so I couldn't move. I was struggling to get away when a hand on my shoulder brought me out of it. I looked up to see Nancy smiling at me.

"I brought your mail," she said. "There's even a card for me."

"Why for you? You're not sick!"

She started reading. "It says right here, 'Mr. *and Mrs. Bull.*'"

It was true that the newspaper captions often referred to her as "Mrs. Bull," and some of the players called her that. Nancy got along great with the players and the press.

When I was finally released from the hospital, I went almost directly to the Boston training camp, my incision still oozing. Unable to throw myself immediately into my usual feverish intensity at practice, I spent my spare time getting into trouble. My constant drinking in the bars near camp and the disturbances I caused gave management the excuse they seemed to be looking for to call me on the carpet. The new coaches had come in late the season before and didn't know much about me as a player. They knew I had ended the season with several painful injuries. When they told me that I didn't fit into their plans for the future, I believed that they had decided to make an example of me in order to keep the other players under control. At the end of the preceding year, I had been voted The Most Valuable Player, but now I didn't fit into their plans.

I was sent to the Green Bay Packers, arriving there four days before the first exhibition game of the '71 season. I had played for them six weeks when Baltimore asked for me. The Packers said they would not give me up; then they put me on waivers. Totally confused by their actions, I went in to see Coach Dan Devine. He looked at me as if he were giving up his best friend and said, "Letting you go is just like letting my own son go." (I could almost hear violins playing in the background.) I looked him in the eye and asked, "Could you really treat your son like this?"

Well, I was gone, I knew that. Some of it, maybe all of it, was my own fault. I knew I had irritated the coach with my clowning around. The only Devine I knew about was Andy Devine, so I called the coach "Jingles" for the character actor. It didn't help endear me to him.

I played the clown everywhere I went. I have often told people that the only book I ever read from start to finish was *The Clown At Second Base*, which was basically true. Now that I understand myself a little better, I see that I used the clown appeal as a defensive maneuver in dealing with difficult situations. When I was growing up, the things that happened could have kept me crying all the time; getting caught in the middle with no way out is tragic to a little kid. I just learned to tell myself that I didn't care—then I put on my act to prove it.

Going back to Memphis during football season was hard, and having to explain it to people made it even harder. I usually answered, "I don't understand it, either," though I was less baffled than I ever admitted. It is still true today that no matter how valuable I may consider something, its cost to me can make it expendable. I am sure that was more or less the case in every instance of my leaving a team.

I didn't talk about it at home, but I still had not given up on football. Neither had Nancy. Several games into the season, Tommy Nobis of the Atlanta Falcons was injured, and Coach Norm Van Brocklin called me up.

"I need a good linebacker," he told me, "and I think you're my man. You will have to play some on the kick-off team."

I didn't hesitate. "Fine with me, Coach. It's gotta' be somebody's job. I'll help you any way I can."

When reporters asked Nancy how she felt about the call, she answered, "Delighted! This is John's game—and it really is his life."

"So you didn't mind getting his bags out and packing them?"

Nancy laughed. "Are you kidding? I never unpacked them."

I was given No. 62. After I had been in Atlanta a couple of Sundays, a teammate called my attention to a sign in the stands. It read, "Watch No. 62." The Atlanta fans called me "Bull" and chanted it when I went down to tear into the blocking wedge after the kick-off. People who think the fans are not important to the game are crazy. I have seen the momentum change radically just on the mood of the crowd. The Atlanta fans were great. They could really fire the players up. But once the play started, I didn't need extra incentive.

A wedge buster has to have speed and momentum. When I ran down field full speed and threw my body into those players out in front of the kick returner, I used every ounce of force in my body. I thought our chances to be a winning team looked good.

For every game the Falcons won, Coach Van Brocklin gave his own personal trophy, the "Golden Jock" award, to the player who contributed most. The award was a bronzed replica of a jock strap. I won it against New Orleans and again for a Monday night game against the Green Bay Packers. In the Packers' game, I broke two face masks, a jaw, and a collar bone. After the game, two Packer coaches came over to me and said, "We told them it was a mistake to let you go." I felt better after that, but I still resented the way the Packers had handled my situation.

I settled into the specialty teams play even though I wanted to be out there every game as a linebacker. I knew I had some good men ahead of me who were there long before I came: Greg Brezina, Ron Acks, and Don Hansen. I appreciated a chance to play.

Two games remained in the season when my knee took the blow that was actually the decisive factor in ending my football career. We were playing in Minnesota on a field that was frozen hard. I threw a block, and as I hit a man in mid-air, I lost control of my body. My right leg whiplashed against the ice. I felt the cartilages pop. When I tried to get up, I realized that they had popped out of the knee socket. I reached down and was able somehow to push them back inside the socket. I found that I could still run, so I finished the game. After every play, I would push those cartilages back into place. When I ran, they popped right back out again. By the time the team returned to Atlanta, my knee was the size of my head. By morning it was obvious that my 1971 season was over. I would have to have an operation to put my right knee back in working order.

Every injured athlete knows that the surgery isn't the toughest part; it is the rehabilitation period while the body heals and regains strength. I had gone through it so many times before that every phase was fresh in my mind. I had played my entire career at 205 pounds, a very light weight for my position. When people commented on my intensity, I knew they didn't realize what I was up against. When you're trying to stop guys the size of some of those NFL players, you know the only way you're going to do it is to put something extra into your hitting.

I knew when I was clearing out my locker at the end of the season that before another began, I had some serious thinking to do. In my locker I found a stack of pictures of myself in uniform which management provided; all the players had them so they could give signed copies to their fans. I looked up and saw Greg Brezina cleaning out his locker, so I took one of my pictures, wrote a note on it, and signed my name. Then I took it over to

Greg. He read it and burst out laughing. I had written, "To Greg Brezina from "Bull" Bramlett. Maybe some day you will be as good a linebacker as I am. 'Bull.'"

Greg had been my roommate on the road while I played for the Falcons. He was a new Christian. He read his Bible a lot and often talked to me about it. I knew enough "religion" from my church-going days on Alabama Street to carry on a conversation about it, so I sometimes led him on a little, though I never really listened.

The note I wrote on my picture was in keeping with the kind of kidding that goes on among ball players. Greg was a fine line-backer and he knew I respected him. I expected him to pitch the picture into a wastebasket after I left. It was a year and half later that I found out what he actually did with it.

Hanging up the cleats was not as tough as I had expected. In May 1972 I announced my retirement from football. I was almost certain it would come to that after the injury in Minnesota. I had played seven years, missing only four games. During that time, I had sustained six knee operations. I would have liked to believe that I could still play, but deep down I knew that if I expected to remain active, my body had taken its limit of punishment. Nancy had suffered too through all the times I was hurt, and I knew she was anxious for me to give it up.

Looking back, I'm sure Nancy had no idea what was ahead. If coming home to stay had any effect at all, it was to intensify my undisciplined actions. When I wasn't working, I was hanging out at night, drinking and fighting and giving Nancy and the boys a bad time when I was at home.

After my Dixiemart Corondolet job, I had worked with Bank Americard, calling on those who fell behind on credit card pay-ments. I am sure they hired me because of my "tough" image without realizing that my sympathies lay with the overextended debtors. I knew what it was like to be poor. On one occasion, I was sent out to pick up the credit card of a widow with several chil-dren. That one visit convinced me that in order to make a living, I was going to need a different job; not only did I leave without the credit card, but my wallet was several dollars lighter.

Before retiring from football, I had already begun working for a fire alarm company, and the job was waiting for me when I got back to Memphis. I was interested in the selling end of business, so I went into it full time with great enthusiasm. I did well selling and in leading sales meetings.

We had been home for about a year when a friend of Nancy's, Susan Brooks, asked her to join a Bible study that Trish Fulghum was teaching. After that, everything began to change for Nancy. It was as if she had found a new world, one that I didn't share. She spent a great deal of time reading the Bible and playing tapes of sermons and religious music. She joined Bible Study Fellowship and tried to share with me, but I didn't want to listen, so after awhile she laid low. The change in her that puzzled me most was the happiness she seemed to have found in spite of the turmoil I stirred up. When I told myself that this change in her would have no effect on me, I should have realized after fourteen years of marriage that when she believed in something, I was going to hear more about it.

I suspected she spent a lot of time praying, and it wasn't hard to figure out who most of it was for. Her increasing confidence triggered anger in me. When I threw things around and yelled obscenities at her, it seemed to roll off like water from a duck's back. I knew how she hated for me to hang out in the rough joints, so after every temper fit, I headed for the nearest beer joint.

I wanted to call attention to the way I lived as if embarrassing Nancy was the only way I could get back at her for what I considered her disloyalty to me. I had never seen any good come out of religion. My father could go to church, read the Bible, and pray out of one side of his mouth while he cursed you out of the other. He could always spare a few minutes from his religion to jerk a lamp cord loose and lay it across your back till it brought blood. One blow from his bony knuckles could bust your lip wide open or close an eye. So I didn't want to hear from Nancy any of that stuff I associated with religion. We'd made it this far, and I didn't like the idea she seemed to have that we needed to change.

I was making plans to attend a seminar connected with my job, and I knew Nancy was hoping I would change my mind and stay home. She knew the week would end in a wild drinking binge. I made a point of telling her what a great time I was going to have. She knew how useless it would be to argue with me so she just packed my bag and wished me luck with my golf game. Several others were going along to do some golfing.

While I was away that week, I tried every outrageous thing I could think of to keep from thinking. One day I was carrying my beer around the golf course, iced down in a waste basket from the motel. I had my golf clubs in one hand, my beer in the other. Toward the end of the course, I got hot. I just stopped and began shedding my clothes. I played the last three holes of golf naked as a skinned skunk. The other fellows on the course were getting such a kick out of me, I just crawled up on the hood of the car and straddled it for the ride back to the motel. I can't remember if we met anyone on the ride, but if we did, I'm sure the shock of seeing me as a hood ornament had an unsettling effect. Jekyll Island was probably never the same after my week's stay there.

Soon afterward, I went with some of the men from work to Augusta, Georgia, for the Masters Golf Tournament. We stayed in South Carolina and played golf for a few days. I stayed drunk and ran the streets, getting into everything I could. Along with my liquor, I was popping pills. I slept only about five hours the entire week. I made it to the Masters' once, on the last day.

On our way home, I was talking to Ed Rotenberry, one of the men who went. "I push hard, everything I do," I said. I felt that I needed to explain my actions, but more to myself than to anyone else; "I believe in living flat out. Just pull out all the stops."

He grinned. "Well, you do that," he agreed.

"No, I mean it, there's a reason why I feel that way. You know, Ed, I'm going to die young. I really believe it."

Ed disagreed. "No, I don't buy that. You can't know that. Nobody knows."

"I do. I've been thinking about it. But I know this, I'm not going to sit around waiting for it to happen."

Thoughts of death had been creeping into my mind at the oddest times, like right in the middle of watching a ball game. Or maybe I'd wake up in the night with a depression I couldn't shake. I knew subconsciously that the odds were against someone who drank and fought as much as I did.

When I got home from Augusta, Nancy tried to ask about my trip, but I was too drunk to talk. I fell across the bed asleep. When I got out of bed the next morning to get ready for work, my head felt like it had a jackhammer inside it. I staggered into the bathroom and there on the mirror were huge letters written in lipstick. I shut my eyes and opened them again, trying to focus. The glaring red letters were still there, spelling out what was undoubtedly Nancy's message to me: *GOD IS GOING TO GET YOU!* I left without talking to her.

After work, I went to the 'Y' to work out. When I opened my gym bag, there was a note on top of my clothes. It said: "Jesus loves you, but He is still going to get you." It was becoming increasingly clear that my wife was not going to remain content to enjoy her newfound "relationship to Christ" all by herself. She had one convert in mind, and I was beginning to suspect that I was it. I left the 'Y' and went to one of my favorite joints for a drink.

Nancy knew all the places I hung out because I had caused a few disturbances in most of them. When I stumbled out to my car that night after the bar closed, there on the steering wheel, taped down, was a note. Under the street light, I could barely make out the words, GOD LOVES YOU, BUT HE IS DEFINITELY GOING TO GET YOU!

It seemed that the faster I ran to escape my thoughts, the more I was confronted by incidents involving those whose line of thinking opposed mine. Every way I turned, I was seeing or hearing something about religion.

Linda Parish came over to invite Nancy to a revival in her church, and Nancy immediately began pleading with me to go with her. It seemed so important to her to expose me to more religion, I agreed to go. I decided that was a good way to get all of this unwanted attention stopped; I'd just pick a night, go, and get it over.

The whole family went, and Nancy was happy. I got out of there without getting into any embarrassing situations. The preacher was warm and friendly, the people were warm and friendly—and I was, too. Now, Nancy could ease up on me. Mission accomplished.

I was sitting in the living room with a can of beer watching television one night when the doorbell rang. Nancy went to the door. The two men standing there introduced themselves as members of the church where we had attended the revival. I heard her invite them in and said to myself, *Uh-oh, those Christians have come to get me.* I set my beer over behind the sofa and braced myself to receive some more religion.

The men, Ron Young and Ken Meador, were very pleasant and friendly. It was a short visit. I kept waiting for them to start talking about the bad things I did, and I was certain they would eventually tell me how I ought to live. None of that ever came up. They talked instead about the way they lived in respect to Jesus. They spoke of Jesus as a real person who had changed them from hopelessly lost drifters into saved men, at peace with themselves.

Ken suddenly turned to me and asked, "John, are you a Christian?"

"Uh . . . I've been b'ptised," I eked out.

He began talking, giving a personal testimony of what Jesus had done in his life, and I found something happening that I had never experienced before. I was actually listening to what he had to say. I glanced over at Nancy, sitting quietly beside me, and saw tears in her eyes. I thought, *she is probably scared to death that I'm going to get up and throw these guys out of here.*

This visit was not going as I had expected. These men were not blowing smoke; they were not spouting self-righteous doctrine. If they sounded a little over confident, they were obviously not bragging on themselves. They made it very clear that they considered Jesus the answer to everything.

When Ron and Ken were leaving, Ron turned at the door and looked back at me. "John, do you know why we came by here tonight?"

"No, not really. Why?"

Looking straight into my eyes, he answered, "We came for one reason: John, we love you."

I don't know what I said then. Those four words, "John, we love you," caught me by surprise. After they walked out the door, I stood there turning the words over in my mind. No man had ever told me he loved me. The words hit me with a disturbing sense of shock. The turmoil inside me demanded some kind of action, so I went over and picked up my can of beer behind the couch.

16

Another Chance

It was dark outside the kitchen window. I stood there staring out, still holding the can of beer in my hand as I thought about the two men who had just left my home. Not quite sure why I did it, I suddenly turned the can upside down in the sink. It felt good. I opened the refrigerator and took out all the cans I had there. I opened them and poured the beer into the sink. Then I went to the cabinet where I kept the liquor and began removing it. I emptied all of it as well.

Nancy stood in the door watching me. She was crying, but I didn't ask why. I didn't stop what I was doing. When I had finished pouring out the liquor, I sacked up all the bottles and cans and carried them outside to the trash barrel.

Maybe the normal thing to have done would have been to talk, I don't know. I had always been so opinionated, biased actually, about everything and everybody that it seemed strange to suddenly find myself totally confused. Nancy went to the couch and sat down as if she wanted to be close by in case I wanted to let her in on what I was thinking. But I didn't know what to think. I sat down in a chair and closed my eyes. The questions I had were not the kind that others could answer: not Nancy and not the two men who had talked to me about a Savior.

Why had they come? "We came for one reason: John, we love you." But to me, their reason only raised a bigger question: Why did they love me? They didn't know me, and nothing they knew about me could possibly give them a reason to love me. And why did they tell those personal experiences that I wouldn't be able to talk openly about if they happened to me? And how could they be so sure that what they believed was true? All of these questions were demanding answers that I didn't have. I opened my eyes and saw that Nancy had left the room. I picked up her Bible and opened it. Flipping through it, I started reading.

"Ye have heard that it hath been said, An eye for an eye, and a tooth for a tooth."* I could relate to that. I read on. "But I say unto you, That ye resist not evil: but whosoever shall smite thee on thy right cheek, turn to him the other also."¹ I stopped. Who could do that?

When I came to the verse that asks, "For if ye love them which love you, what reward have ye?"² I stopped again. Under the rules implied here, who could be loved? Who would waste time loving those who don't care about you? I went on reading. I agreed with all that stuff about good deeds being done for show. It always steamed me when a man could take his family to church, then go home and beat his kids and slap his wife around.

I'd always been able to mumble over the Lord's Prayer in a group, so I skimmed over that. I got a little hung up on the verses following it that emphasized forgiveness. They seemed to be saying that this was the important point of the whole prayer. You'd have to know some of the people I knew firsthand, especially the religious ones, to understand my view of forgiveness. How can you forgive someone who thinks he is always right and never admits a need for forgiveness?

I don't know how long I read. Nancy and the boys were asleep and I knew it was very late, but I was looking for something that would clear up some of the questions in my mind. I finally found a clue to my respect for what Ron Young and Ken Meador had said, in spite of my skepticism. I came across the passage by accident, though I should have suspected by then that nothing about the entire evening was accidental. "Whosoever believeth that Jesus is the Christ is born of God: and every one that loveth him that begat loveth him also that is begotten of him."³

Neither Ron nor Ken had tried to build himself up. Both had just told how great it is to know Jesus. They believed He loved them. Because of that, they loved me. They weren't talking what I labeled religion, but Jesus Christ. This was something entirely different from what I had believed. I decided to sleep on it.

I woke up promptly at 6 a.m. and lay there watching Nancy sleep. With her hair loose around her face, she looked like a little girl. Something about seeing her that way was depressing to me. I thought, *this is the woman I have shoved and slapped around for fourteen years.* Looking at her as she lay there defenseless made the sudden flashback on my temper fits unbearable, so I got up and went to work. I left without talking to anyone, but as I passed the chair I had spent most of the night in, I picked up the Bible.

I wasn't out of my office much that day. A few people came in, but by mid-afternoon everything was quiet. I closed my office door and opened the Bible. "Moreover, brethren, I declare unto you the gospel which I preached unto you, which also ye have received, and wherein ye stand; By which also ye are saved . . . ."[4]

I was reading at random. I read the entire fifteenth chapter of 1 Corinthians, all about a risen Christ who overcame death, and how in Him, all who are His are made alive. I didn't know who wrote it, but he said he laid his life on the line every day for his faith because of his certainty in the Lord Jesus. I couldn't stop reading. I couldn't grasp the meaning of a lot of it, but every few verses I'd come across something about myself. I got so curious that I started looking at the beginning of the part I was reading to see who wrote it. I came to a startling revelation: the Apostle Paul knew "Bull" Bramlett.

I went home after work still thinking about the guts of this man in standing for what he believed. He wasn't pulling any punches when he said, "Know ye not that the unrighteous shall not inherit the kingdom of God? Be not deceived: neither fornicators, nor idolaters, nor adulterers, nor effeminate, nor abusers of themselves with mankind, nor thieves, nor covetous, nor drunkards, nor revilers, nor extortioners, shall inherit the kingdom of God."[5]

Any place I turned in the Bible, I could see "Bull" Bramlett. The more I saw, the worse I felt. I continued reading, as if the key to the only way I could feel better was somewhere in those pages.

The next night, I read through almost the entire New Testament. Much of it was triggering painful memories, incidents from my past that I hated remembering.

Some of the buried ghosts involved Nancy, but most went further back—punishment for childish misconduct, resulting in most instances in brutal punishment. Still clear in my mind after all the years, the details contradicted what I was finding in the pages of this book. I was trying to understand a heavenly Father who loves and forgives, with nothing in my experience as a son to recommend Him.

I avoided talking to Nancy. She tried at first to draw me into conversation, then just fell in with my mood and went on with her chores. I asked where the boys were, and she answered briefly, "Staying all night with Mother and Dad."

I went to bed to get away from my thoughts, and then couldn't sleep because of them. I couldn't get past those early years of my life. I was remembering incidents as if they happened yesterday; people I had hurt, all the chances I had blown. All the time I was growing up, resentful of being poor, I dreamed of getting my chance to be somebody. I lay there thinking, *I had my chance. I was given a chance to get an education when I received a scholarship to Memphis State University. I didn't cash it in. I got a chance to play professional baseball. I threw that away. When I got my chance to play pro football, I couldn't even see that my options were running out.*

Could it be possible that I was now being given another chance, a chance at a life that would make me happy? Nothing ever had. Any pleasure I got out of what I did was shortlived, spoiled by my own hostile nature. The longer I lay there staring into the darkness, the more miserable I felt. *Someone must have been watching out for me all the time.* The dangerous situations I had propelled myself into, the explosive circumstances I had created all my life; I suddenly realized how fortunate I was that someone hadn't killed me or that I had not died in an accident.

I almost drowned when I was a scrawny, seven-year-old, in an old bayou behind Winchester Park. I couldn't swim. I had waded out to catch crawfish and stepped off into a deep hole. I went down several times before an older boy, Donald Arnold, came in after me. This is where my younger son's name came from. We had named our first son, Andy, for Nancy's maiden name, Andrews. When Don was born, I named him for the boy who saved me from drowning.

As I lay in bed remembering my past, the thought came to me: *Another chance.* If Donald had not come by the old bayou at just that moment, I would not be here. I suddenly realized the influence of an unseen hand reaching out to stop certain destruction. How many times had He intervened? Where would I be, I wondered, if I had made the most of just half the chances I had been given?

I was glad when morning came. If one thing had come out of wrestling with my past all night, it was the decision to forget it and go on with my life. Looking at my face in the mirror as I shaved, I knew it wasn't going to work. Instead of forgetting, all the hurt I had inflicted on others was magnifying itself in my mind. *Go ahead, God, stack it all up, I did it all. My wife and my little boys think they know a lot, but they don't know half the things I've done. Those men who thought You could save me, Ron Young, and Ken Meador—they don't know what I've done. But You do, God. And I do. And I don't blame You if it's too much to forgive.*

I don't know how I got through the morning. I must have spoken with people at work, I don't remember. I finally closed my office door. I sat down with the weight of thirty-one years of wrong direction on my shoulders and a little *Christian Life New Testament* in my hand which Ron had given me earlier that week.

I opened it to the beginning and began to study the outline for dealing with sin. I saw sin for what it was and what it was was me. Hey, I'd done it all; not only transgressing God's law, but by staying in that perpetual state, I had made myself His enemy. God had a remedy for sin, but I didn't understand what I was to do after reading it. "For he hath made him to be sin for us, who knew no sin that we might be made the righteousness of God in him."[6] I felt a deep hunger to know Him. I wanted His forgiveness for all the unrightness in me. I wanted to drink from that well that Jesus told the Samaritan woman of, because nothing I had known up to now was going to satisfy the thirst I had. If I had to be made a new man to have the "living water," I'd do it—I was sick enough of the old one.

Looking down at the open book in my hand, I read, "For God so loved the world, that he gave his only begotten Son, that whosoever believeth in him should not perish, but have everlasting life."[7] Whosoever? Jesus died for "whosoever"? That could be me!

I fell down on my knees there by my desk and cried out to the same God I had been running from. I asked Him to forgive me for being what I was, for throwing away all the chances He had given me to know Him. I had finally come to the point of knowing that this was the only chance that mattered. I said, *"God, if You can make anything You can use from this rotten, stinking, reprobate drunk, I want You to take me."*

When I got up off my knees I was saved, but I had only a vague notion of what it all meant. I wanted to live for Jesus, and I wanted to glorify Him. I wanted to show everybody in the whole world what Jesus could do for a confirmed sinner like me, and I wanted to do it right then! I wanted to start living a new life, but I had no idea how to go about it. I didn't even realize that letting Jesus come into my heart was only the beginning.

I looked at the calendar on my desk. May 25, 1973. I saw by the clock that only a few minutes had lapsed since I was miserable and confused, hating myself but not knowing any other way. Now I was experiencing a love unlike anything I had ever known. I was released from fear and anger and was able to experience the peace of God's presence, all in a matter of seconds. Tears of joy were streaming down my face. I just had to tell somebody. I opened the door and called my secretary.

"You know what? I just got saved."

"Saved from what?" she asked.

I couldn't wait to share the news with Ron and Ken. I called them at their offices. They got excited. Both told me they had been praying for me since the night they visited in our home.

I called "Doc" Eshleman. I had refused his wise counsel when he spoke in chapel services for the Dolphins while I was playing ball in Miami, but I never doubted his sincerity. He was happy to hear that I had finally opened my heart to the mighty Savior.

I thought of Greg Brezina, who had tried to witness to me in Atlanta. I called his home. His wife, Connie, told me I could reach him at his office and gave me the number. When I got him on the phone, I didn't waste time on small talk.

"Greg," I said, "This is Bull—Bull Bramlett. I want to tell you, something has just happened. Man, the Lord Jesus just saved me!"

"Bull, you mean right now?"

"Yeah, man, just a few minutes ago."

Greg shouted out, "Praise the Lord!" The sincere joy in his voice got to me, and I started crying. I tried to tell him how good it felt to have Jesus in my heart, but I had nothing to compare it to. Nothing had ever felt that good before. When we calmed down, Greg asked me if I remembered the picture I gave him when I left the Falcons.

I laughed, remembering the message I had written on it. "Yeah, Greg, I sure do."

"Do you know what I did with that picture, Bull?"

"I've no idea."

"I taped it to my locker," he said. "I want you to know, Bull, I have been praying for you every day since then. I'm just glad to know that God is still in the prayer-answering business."

A year and a half had passed since I had seen or spoken with him. But Greg Brezina, although busy with his football career and his family, without my knowing it had taken the time to pray for me every day. After I got off the phone, I thought about that. I couldn't take in all I had suddenly become a part of. The power of prayer. Back when I was at my worst, Nancy had said one night before I left the house, "John, I can't stop you from all that you are doing, but I want you to know I am praying for you. And I am not the only one." No doubt she had all the women in her Bible study group praying for me. Ron Young and Ken Meador had prayed for me. I had no idea how many others, all praying for me to know the Lord. It was an awesome realization. I started crying again.

In our home that night, Nancy and I celebrated. Our boys may not have fully understood what had happened, but they knew the atmosphere under our roof had changed. They knew I had changed. Nancy and I were laughing, crying, trying to tell each other how we felt. We marvelled at the love we suddenly had for each other. We were overwhelmed by the love of Jesus for us, giving up His life on a cruel cross so we could know Him and have everlasting life. We talked, choked up, then just held each other, the four of us. Then we cried some more. I tell you it was awesome! All of this was going on between telephone conversations. Nancy and I had so many to share the good news with: Ad and "Pop," my mom, Linda and Paul Parish, and other friends who had shown their concern for us over the years. When I talked with my mother, I heard her voice break as she told me how long she had been praying for all of her boys. Because I had constantly been in trouble, I suspected she had felt that she had to pray extra hard for me. I was so glad to be able to assure her that God had answered her prayers for me.

It was well after midnight before we settled down. Andy and Don finally wore out and went to sleep, leaving us with our Bible open, still reading and talking. And praying. What a night! No newborn baby ever got a better reception into a family than reborn "Bull" Bramlett received that night in his own home.

17

"You're Not Bull Bramlett!"

"How do you feel this morning?" Nancy asked. We were sitting at the table drinking coffee the morning after my conversion. I didn't even have to think about it. "Like a new man," I answered.

I knew when I walked out the door and went to work that everything was going to be different. I had no idea how different. The full impact had not yet hit me.

I didn't know much about praying, but as I drove to work, I talked to Jesus. I said, "Lord, you know I've been stirred up about something all my life. Now this is the biggest thing that ever happened to me. I don't want to be all fired up one minute, then ready to back off the next. You didn't do that. I don't want to have religion. I want to be changed from what I was."

I knew in my heart that I was already different, but I had seen too many people become emotionally excited, then lose interest. I never did that playing ball and I didn't want to do it now.

I had not anticipated other people's reaction to me. Until they saw me it was hard for them to believe I had changed. A man who had known me for years told me later that when I walked into his business after my conversion, he noticed immediately that something about me was different. He said my countenance was actually altered. I was unaware of it, though I knew my attitude toward people changed immediately. Those I had resented, I began to love. The things I had loved to do, I now hated. And it was not a conscious effort; I really felt it. I could never have made myself hate booze, fighting, and carousing. God did it. The love of Jesus filled me so full of joy and peace that if I heard his name or saw it printed somewhere, my eyes filled with tears. I could speak his name and bring on a flood! It was so exciting to know Jesus.

Nancy and I weighed our next decision carefully. I had been made a new man, and all indications pointed toward our making a break with everything concerning the old life. So I left my job selling fire alarm systems.

Joining the unemployed was not nearly as difficult as it would have been had I known what would follow. A good salary had accustomed us to living with better-than-average accommodations. Our idea that God would step in and provide a position which would further my Christian growth wasn't happening, for reasons of His own, I am sure. The savings went, Nancy's Lincoln and my Olds went, and we could no longer afford the things we had taken for granted.

I went without a job for five months. I was busy every day, but there was no paycheck. When I look back on those times of trying to stretch every penny to the limit, it was rough, but all through it Nancy and I were experiencing the grace of God in a hundred different ways. We were getting to know each other in ways we never had. I was learning to love my sons in ways that would honor God, teaching them to love Jesus. And we were all learning to have fun together. Like the woman at the well, I wanted others to know I had met Christ and that He was real.

My next-door neighbor, Mr. Ray, was a cop. I didn't talk to him about Jesus. In fact, I didn't talk to him at all unless it was absolutely necessary. I didn't like him. I had been in jails all over the country from Homestead, Florida, to Minneapolis, Minnesota, and I didn't like any cop. I thought they gave me trouble everywhere I went, and I had a particular grudge against Mr. Ray.

Two years before, Nancy and I had given Andy and Don go-carts for Christmas. Bright and early on Christmas morning, the boys were running their go-carts around in the cove when two cops knocked on our door. I was still in bed, hung over from the night before. The police told Nancy I had to get those kids off the street with their go-carts.

She woke me up. "John, you've got to get up. Two policemen are here to talk to you about the noise the boys are making."

I started growling about getting disturbed. "I'll go in there and take care of the noise. I'll just have to whip me a cop. That will stop it."

"John, you can't do that. Now please, don't start something. You're just going to mess up another Christmas! You're going to get yourself thrown in jail."

I went to the door and asked, "What's the problem?"

One of them said, "Your boys are making too much noise with their go-carts. You're going to have to get them off the streets."

"All right," I said.

I went out and called Andy and Don to come in. After the cops left, I told the boys to get back out there. I believed that Mr. Ray next door was the one who called the cops about my boys.

After that, I began to think of ways to get even with Mr. Ray without getting caught. Every time I got drunk, I'd plan how I could put a stocking over my head and catch him out in a dark alley some night.

After I became a Christian, I stopped that, but I had not grown enough to deal voluntarily with all the harmful emotions in my life. I just avoided people I didn't like so I wouldn't have to deal with my feelings.

I had just walked inside my house one day when Mr. Ray pulled up next door. The Spirit of God spoke to me and said, "John, you've been telling everybody you see about the Lord, but you haven't told him yet."

In my heart I answered, "I'm not going to tell him either." I went on, reminding the Lord of what that man did to my boys on Christmas Day. I said, "That was your Son's birthday, and that man called the cops on those little boys."

The Spirit spoke back, "John, do you love me?"

I said, "Lord, you know I love you. Nobody else has ever been able to do with me, to me, and for me, what you've done. Yes, Lord, I love you."

In my heart, He said, "How can you say you love me, when

you hate that cop? You've never seen me, and you see that cop every day."

The words of 1 John 4:20 popped into my mind, "If a man saith, I love God, and hateth his brother, he is a liar; for he that loveth not his brother whom he hath seen, how can he love God whom he has not seen?" I said, "Lord, you've got me there. That's right."

So I opened the door and walked out to meet Mr. Ray. I walked up to him and said, "Mr. Ray, I've never liked you, but I have become a Christian. I've given my heart to Jesus and I want you to know, Mr. Ray, that I love you." As I told him about the two men coming to my home to tell me about Christ, I choked up. When I started crying, he did too.

"John," he said, "I became a Christian when I was thirteen years old, but I haven't lived the way I should." He thanked me for talking to him and said, "I'm going to get back in church Sunday, John, and I'm going to start living for the Lord." He did it!

The Lord had begun uncovering my prejudices. I had had so much trouble with cops, I guess He figured that was the place to start. After that worked out so well, He went right after me on another trouble spot.

I didn't like the long-haired, bearded, hippie look. Actually, that is an understatement; anything bordering on that look gave me an excuse to start a fight. In North Memphis where I grew up, everyone wore short hair and shaved. Elvis made the greased-back style popular, but the neat look was the only one acceptable to me. I was driving down the expressway one day when I saw a hitchhiker trying to catch a ride. He looked terrible in a dirty tee shirt and blue jeans. He had a long beard and long hair hanging down his back. As I drove closer to him, the Spirit of God spoke inside me and said, "Hey, you need to pick up this hippie."

I'm saying, "Naw, wait a minute. You've got me to loving cops. You mean I've got to love this hippie too?"

He said, "Yeah, John, you've got to love this hippie, too." I pressed down hard on the accelerator. As soon as I had passed on by, I said, "Lord, I was going too fast—I couldn't stop in time to pick him up. But, I'll start doing what You want, Lord. I will sure pick up the next one." The Lord wouldn't leave me alone about it, so I cut off on the next exit, returned to the freeway, and started back. All the way around, I was hoping the hippie would be gone because I still didn't want to pick him up. If I could have done what I wanted, I would probably have stopped and whipped him because of his looks.

Of course, he was still there. I stopped and opened the car door. When he got in, I looked behind him to see where the goats were. The smell was so bad I rolled down my window and turned up the air conditioner full blast. I began talking with him about the Lord, then I noticed how skinny he was. I asked, "Son, how long has it been since you had something to eat?"

"About ten days, I think, since I had a meal."

"How long since you had a bath?"

"About two weeks."

He could have said two years and I would have believed him. As I drove along, I felt that I ought to do more than just take him a few miles down the road. I began to think about taking him home with me. It was getting close to noon, so I just turned and headed for home.

Nancy was standing in the doorway when we got out of the car, and I am sure she thought, *What in the world is this man going to do next?* But she didn't bat an eye. Her life with me had always been filled with the unexpected. She could see that the boy needed food, so she fixed a big lunch for us.

Afterward I asked him, "Son, would you like to get a haircut?"

"Yes, sir, I would."

I took him down to a barber shop before I remembered that Memphis barber shops were closed on Mondays. I said, "Don't worry about it, I know how to cut hair, and I can shave you too."

I took him into our bathroom and started to work on him. I gave Nancy his clothes to burn. When I got that long hair off and began to get into his beard, I couldn't believe what I saw. Ticks had burrowed into his scalp and into his face under the beard. There were so many of them, I'm sure they had sucked a lot of blood out of him. After I got him cleaned up and dressed in some of my clothes, we discovered a nice looking boy under all that mess.

While that young man talked with us, the Lord impressed upon me the tragedy of the hundreds of thousands of young people who are running from God without knowing where they are going. They may be running because of parents who don't take time for them or from someone who abuses them—or maybe they are trying to find someone to give them an anchor on which they can hold. It is hard to believe that anyone would leave a home where they feel loved.

I told the boy that I wanted to help him, that I had two sons of my own and he could be the third. "I'll find you a job and you can stay here with us."

He said, "Mr. Bramlett, I appreciate that, but I have a job waiting for me in Miami. I'll be all right when I get there. I need to get down there as soon as I can." He wanted to go, so Nancy packed a bag for him with clothes, a Bible, and some sandwiches. I took him down to the expressway to catch a ride. As he got out of the car, I asked, "Son, do you have any money?"

"No, sir, but I'll be okay now."

I had a five dollar bill in my pocket, and I gave it to him. He reached out and grabbed my arm. Looking straight into my eyes, he said, "Mr. Bramlett, I want you to know, I love you."

Those words went all over me. I felt that this was God's way of telling me that I needed to be helping all the young people I could, including the hitchhikers. They needed to hear about Jesus, to be told what He could make of their lives. Many of the young people I see who are in trouble are looking for happiness the same way I was. Like me, they need someone to show them who can give it to them.

This young man already knew the Lord. What he needed right then was encouragement to use the belief he had. When Nancy found out I was making a practice of picking up hitchhikers, she lectured me. "I hear constantly of people being robbed, or worse. John, you are going to get killed. It is dangerous to stop for people you don't know. I wish you wouldn't do it."

"You worry too much," I said. "If they rob me, what are they going to get?"

Not long after this, phone calls began coming in from parents all around the country, thanking us for helping their children by giving them rides and talking to them about what they should do. Strangely, Nancy got every one of those calls; I have never received one. The Lord was saying to her, "Leave that fool alone. I'll take care of him."

One day I picked up a hitchhiker who didn't respond to my witness in quite the way I had expected or hoped; in fact, he let me know that he was a homosexual. I began telling him what the Bible says about homosexuality, and he didn't want to hear it. He told me to pull over and let him out. When I complied, I said, "Look, Bud, I just want you to know, I love you." He turned and stuck his head back inside the car. Grinning at me, he said, "Well, I love you too!" Then he took off. I hope he believed me when I told him that he could be set free from homosexuality in the same way we are freed from other sins, but it is hard to convince a man that Jesus can set him free if he doesn't want to be free.

When God saved me, He gave me a specific call right then. I knew He saved me from Hell, but He called me for a purpose, and I began telling people about it. Some of them already knew what that meant, but God called me to tell the ones who had no idea what He could mean to them. I went out looking for those who didn't know Jesus. I'd talk to neighbors on the way to their mailboxes; I even asked kids who came over to play with my boys if they knew the Lord. Those who had known me before probably thought at first that I had become a religious fanatic from being hit in the head too often while playing football or fighting.

Knowing I needed instruction, the Lord began putting godly men in my path. The men who had witnessed to me that night in my home made themselves available to me. Ken took me to *Mid-South Bible College* and introduced me to Dr. James B. Crichton, a brilliant Bible teacher who was president of the college at that time. In honor of him, Mid-South was renamed *Crichton College* in 1987. I began attending Dr. Crichton's Bible class for businessmen, a class that met each Friday morning from six-thirty to seven-thirty.

The first time I heard Dr. Crichton teach, I realized how little Bible doctrine I knew. The subject of predestination came up soon after I joined the class. I was struggling with the principle of election as we studied the book of Romans. Dr. Crichton gave me an explanation that leaves no excuse for a Christian to neglect his opportunity to witness. He said, "One of these days we will leave this world. When we pass through the gates of Heaven, we will look up and there at the entrance will be the words, 'Whosoever will, may come.' When we have walked through the gates, looking back, we will see the words, 'Chosen from the foundation of the world.'"

I said, "Man, Hallelujah!"

He continued, "John, let me tell you this. Remember, you are not responsible for God's decrees. But you are responsible for His commandments."

That settled it for me. There is much I will never understand, but His commandments are clear. To me, He has said, "Bramlett, go into all the world and preach the gospel. Be a witness unto me in Jerusalem, in Judea, in Samaria and to the ends of the earth. *You* tell people about Jesus. Bramlett, *you* just love God and live for Him—and let everybody else argue about the obscure meanings hidden in Scripture. You are responsible for My commandments."

Nancy and I joined a little church near where we lived. Soon afterward, the pastor left for another field and an interim pastor came. I have believed ever since that God arranged this for me. Jesse Newton, an elderly preacher, who had retired from the active ministry, was the pastor Nancy and I needed as babes in Christ. The love of Jesus was reflected in his eyes and on his face. He preached great sermons, but what he said from the pulpit spoke no more clearly than his walk with the Lord. I grew to love Jesse Newton as a friend in Christ, and this taught me an important lesson for any person, saved or lost. When advice is needed, go to someone close to the Savior; not only will he weigh carefully what he tells you, you'll have counsel with the wisdom and power of God behind it.

Jesse is a man of letters; he spoke six languages. His knowledge of Scripture is grounded in an understanding of Greek. He told me what I needed to know in order to preach. He said, "Son, first of all, the way you live in those moments when no one else sees you will determine the way you walk before others. What they see in you will always have a greater effect than anything you might say. If your love for God is genuine, you will never have to search for a message to preach. He has already given you the ultimate sermon for the lost: your own testimony. When you tell others that God can turn hate into love, misery into joy, despair into peace, how can they doubt when living proof stands before them?"

I thanked God for putting Jesse Newton in my path at the very moment I was ready for what he could give me. Talk about timing! If I had been tuned into God's timing when I played professional football, just imagine how many Super Bowl rings I would be wearing today.

In those lean months when I was looking for work, Nancy and I were learning to trust God. The word *faith* gained new meaning when applied to where tomorrow's groceries were coming from. Tomorrow, for Nancy, was a constant concern. Whenever I thought about it, the Spirit of Jesus would speak in my heart: "Hey, you've got Me. Don't worry—I know what I'm doing. 'But seek ye first the kingdom of God, and His righteousness; and all these things shall be added unto you.'"[1]

Soon after I gave my life to Jesus, I began getting invitations from churches and civic organizations to share my testimony with them. One night after I spoke to a Christian Firemen's group, a man approached me. He said, "John, I'm glad to know your life has changed. Vic Scott has told me many incidents of trouble you two used to get into when you played pro baseball together."

Surprised, I asked, "Do you know Vic? Man, I have wondered where he is. Do you know?"

The man explained that he and Vic had worked together for the fire department until Vic had left Memphis some months earlier. "I hear he is back," he said. "I think he is running a beer joint in town."

I was excited. "Just tell me where to find him. I haven't seen Vic in years. I want to tell him what happened to me."

He told me the name of the place. On my way home I felt so impressed to talk to Vic that night that I drove across town to the lounge where he worked. I parked my car and went around to the entrance.

When I got to the door, I stopped. I knew what to expect inside. I had been in a hundred places just like it, but everything was different now. I was not the same man who used to hang out in those places.

The Spirit of God spoke in my heart. "John, don't go in there alone. Go back to your car and get your Bible. If you are going in there, you need to let those people know what you are doing here."

I went back to the car and got the Bible I had used in speaking to the firemen. When I walked into that crowded, noisy bar, it was suddenly as quiet as a funeral parlor. People turned and looked at me standing inside the door with a Bible in my hand, and the whole place seemed to freeze. It was the kind of reaction I might have expected if I had pulled a gun. I walked over to a girl waiting tables and asked for Vic Scott.

"He is not here tonight," she told me, "but you might find out where he is from the man in the back."

I went to the man she pointed out. "I am looking for Vic Scott."

He looked at me and said, "You're John Bramlett."

"Yes, I am. I need to find Vic. I need to tell him something."

"Vic won't be in tonight. I think he went hunting today."

I insisted that I needed to get in touch with him, so he gave me Vic's home telephone number. He told me I could use the phone in the office to call.

When Vic answered the phone, I said, "Vic, this is Bull Bramlett."

He said, "Na-ahh . . . it's not Bull Bramlett."

I said, "Yeah, Vic--this is Bull Bramlett!"

"No. I know Bull Bramlett's voice, and you are not him."

"I am telling you, I am! I called to tell you something. Man, I have given my heart to Jesus, and I want to talk to you."

Very quietly, then, he said, "This is you, ain't it?"

"Yeah."

"Bull, my mama had a full-page story about you from the newspaper and she asked me to read it, but I never did. It was all about you preaching to people and working down at the mission to help people, all that kind of stuff about you becoming a Christian and all of a sudden acting different. The reason I wouldn't read it was because there was no way possible for it to be true. I told her you were a phony. I said, 'There ain't no way Bramlett can be a Christian. I *know* him!'"

"Vic, let me just tell you this. Jesus took everything that was phony in my life and made it real. He changed my life. He changed me, man! That is what I want to talk to you about. I want to talk to you *tonight*, Vic."

"I am not in any shape to talk to anybody tonight," he replied. "Not tonight."

"Okay, Vic, I tell you what I'll do. I'll leave my card here by this phone in your place, and you can call me. I just want you to know, Vic, I love you. And I want to talk to you soon."

He called me the next day and said he wanted to bring his wife, Paula, over to see us. They came that night. Vic's appearance shocked me. He looked as if the world had dealt him a rough hand. Of course, I had not helped by smashing him in the mouth with that lead ball in Raleigh, but there was a look of defeat on his face.

Nancy and I talked about the joy and peace that God had brought into our home, and I could see a hunger in Vic for a better life. When I told him that Jesus said, "I am come that they might have life, and that they might have it more abundantly,"[2] he said, "Man, that's what I want!" Vic made a commitment that night to follow the Lord.

It was exciting to talk about Jesus to those who knew me before

I became a Christian, but I felt a sense of personal failure when I received a negative reaction to my testimony.

Russell Vollmer and I had been teammates at Memphis State University, and after graduation he played football for the Minnesota Vikings. After his career ended, he came home to Memphis and began a successful business venture, Creative Advertising.

I had been a Christian for about six months when I got a surprise telephone call from Russell's wife, Loretta, at 3:30 a.m. When I answered the phone, an unfamiliar voice said, "John, you've never met me, but this is Loretta Vollmer. I'm in trouble, and I need your help. Can you come over to my house?"

It was obvious that she was upset as she explained that she and Russ were on the verge of splitting up. She said enough for me to realize that they needed a lot more than human counsel. Inexperienced as I was at presenting the case for Christianity, I knew I had Jesus in my heart and I knew He had changed me. I had the peace of God, and my life was filled with the joy of knowing Jesus, but I was still trying to learn how to share it with others. I could not even think of Jesus or hear His name without crying. He was so real to me that just saying His name made my emotions spill over.

When I hung up the phone after Loretta's call, I got out of bed, pulled on a tee shirt, bermuda shorts, and a pair of old flip-flops and began gathering up books about the Christian faith, tracts on how to be saved, Bibles, everything about Jesus that I could lay my hands on. I took enough material to save the world.

When I walked in around 4:00 a.m., Russell took one look at me and started laughing. I'm sure it was almost impossible for someone who had known me to believe I could change.

"Well, well," he began, "I heard you got religion."

"No," I said. "I didn't get religion."

"I didn't think you did. I've known you a long time."

I interrupted him, "No, Russell, I didn't get religion. I got Jesus."

He didn't seem to know what to say for a moment, then he asked, "Is it true that you've stopped drinking and running around?"

"Yeah, Russell. It's true."

"You mean you're not getting thrown in jail any more?"

"That's right. I'm not doing any of those things I used to do."

It was too much for Russell to comprehend. "I don't know about this," he said. "I guess I believe some of that stuff about the parting of the waters in the Red Sea, but this is *now*. If God would come down here and do something like that today, or make a building fall down and raise it back up . . . if I could see something like that, then I could believe it."

"Russ," I said, "I see miracles every day."

He raised an eyebrow. "Yeah? Tell me about 'em."

I told him, "Man, you're looking at one right now. This is one of the great privileges God gives today, allowing us to see Him working in the lives of people."

More than anything, even more than I had ever wanted to make the key play in a crucial game, I wanted to help Russ and Loretta know Jesus. So there I sat, trying with everything in me to make them see how it was when Jesus came into my heart. I told them the Scriptures that had spoken to me in my situation. And I cried. For about four hours I just sat there and bawled, telling them about Jesus. They listened, but Russ couldn't bring himself to admit his need. He kept saying, "Loretta has a problem." I finally said, "No, Russell, *you've* got a problem.'"

I felt I had said all I could say, so I went home to give them a chance to think about it. Nancy called Loretta and invited her to church the following Sunday. She didn't go that day, but she went to Nancy's Bible study on Monday, and there she gave her life to Christ. Shortly afterward, Russell attended a Bible study in our home and committed his life to the Lord. Since that time he has been a vital force for Christ in his business, and Loretta works with him to bring their Christian testimony to others. They have a son and two daughters who have been greatly blessed because of Loretta and Russell's willingness to let Jesus change their lives.

When I left their home that morning after sharing my testimony with them, I felt the certainty of God's faithfulness to His promise that "they that sow in tears shall reap in joy."[3] I do remember the happiness Nancy and I shared that following week when the Scripture was literally fulfilled before my eyes: "He that goeth forth and weepeth, bearing precious seed, shall doubtless come again with rejoicing, bringing his sheaves with him."[4] What really mattered about the night I went over to the Vollmers was that God was working out His purposes in His own way.

18

Turning the Corner

During the years I put everything on the line for sports, it never occurred to me that the principle by which I played could be used in serving Christ. The abandonment with which I played the game was the exact, all-out effort the apostle Paul described for the Christian every day: "Know ye not that they which run in a race run all, but one receiveth the prize? So run, that ye may obtain."[1]

But as I studied the whole Word of God, I began to see that this was not the whole story. The Bible also says, "And every man that striveth for the mastery is temperate in all things."* In my intensity to excel on the field, I ignored any suggestion that temperance was to play even a small part in my life. But now that I was living with the Bible as my standard, I set some new rules for myself:

1. To eliminate everything from my character that could slow me down in my run for Jesus.
2. To put out everything I had till the race was over.
3. To trust the mighty God in all things.

It didn't take long for the Lord to go to work on the first of my rules. Excessive pride had governed my nature ever since my first awareness that I was poor. It had eaten at me in school, in my marriage, and in my relationship to anyone in a superior position.

Dr. Adrian Rogers invited me to give my testimony in a Sunday night service at Bellevue Baptist Church. Bellevue's Sunday nights were broadcast over radio, and as my testimony went out over the area, a man sitting in his home fell under Jesus' power to change lives. Jimmy Burell, my brother Charlie's friend, came to

172

me to tell how Jesus had come into his heart as he listened. He said, "John, I know you're having to struggle right now, and I want to help you in a material way." He offered me money, and I said, "No, man, I appreciate it, but I don't need it."

I did need it. I was driving an old, beat-up car that Joe Cooper had given me off his used car lot, and that car would have gone crazy if it had ever seen more than a quarter's worth of gas at one time. Jimmy knew I was going everywhere I could to witness, and out of his gratitude and Christian love, he wanted to help me. He also recognized pride when he saw it, so he started going by my house occasionally to talk with Nancy and the boys. As he left, he'd give Nancy a check "to help take care of some of the ministering expenses." It was definitely needed and greatly appreciated.

I was speaking in churches, clubs, jails, schools, going anywhere I was invited. I have yet to find one without a need for Jesus. At one little church, the pastor came to me after the service and said, "John, some of the ladies want to give you a love offering for your ministry."

I protested. "No, no; I don't want money from anyone for what I'm doing. Just look at what Jesus did for me!"

"Son," he replied, "you're not looking at this in the right way. I saw you put your money in our offering plate, money I suspect you need. May I tell you something?"

"Yes, of course."

"When the Lord sent out his missionaries, he gave them specific instructions to accept offerings. You see, John, these ladies are just trying to return the kindness you've shown them by sharing the gospel. They want to have a part in what you're doing."

I had to admit that I had never seen giving in that light. To me, it had always seemed like charity. I thanked the minister and explained, "It's hard for me to accept money from people I don't even know."

"Son, just so long as you understand why it's hard. If it is pride, you need to change. Remember though, everyone has a need to give and the right to give."

The Lord had zeroed in on my pride. He had begun the tedious

process of weeding it out. Almost immediately, Greg Brezina
called to ask me to come to Atlanta and speak to the Falcons
team. Many of them were men I had played ball with, and I des-
perately wanted to go. I had to admit to Greg that I was financially unable to make the trip. He didn't hesitate. "Bull," he said,
"that is no problem. I'll take care of it." He paid my expenses out
of his own pocket. I was learning. Pride means trouble in every
case; in Kingdom business it brings certain failure because our
whole relationship with Jesus is rooted in His humility.

The Green Bay Packers were playing the Falcons the weekend
I went to Atlanta, so I went over first to their chapel service. I had
played with the Packers for only six weeks, but what they saw of
me in that time must have made what they were hearing about me
now seem incredible. They all came to hear me speak, maybe to
see for themselves that I was not the same "Bull" Bramlett they
knew. Several of them were more than convinced—the Spirit of
God took hold of them and convicted them of their own need to
change. To see these men come to realize the power of God to
change a man's heart was a great thrill to me. I thanked Him that
the work He had done in me was visible, for these former teammates had seen me at my worst.

On the night before a home game, the Falcons stayed at a Holiday Inn outside the city. As I spoke to the players and coaches on
Sunday morning, I believe God used the difference they could see
in me to show them their need to know Him. Decisions were
made to receive Christ, and I thanked the Lord for allowing me to
go back to Atlanta to praise His name. After the game I was in the
locker room. There, on Greg Brezina's locker, was the picture I
had given him. I marveled again at his persistence in prayer. He
had refused to give up on me. I told him, "Man, I thank you for
that. The next time I see a hopeless case, I'm going to think about
how you hung in there praying for me."

At the airport, I was waiting for my flight to Memphis when I
saw a familiar figure go past. I jumped up and ran after him.
"Barry! Barry Brown!" It was Barry all right, my roommate
when I played football with the Patriots. I clotheslined him right

there. Before he could find his voice, I was wringing his hand. I said, "Praise the Lord, Barry, how're you doing?"

He couldn't believe his eyes. He kept saying, "Bull, I know it's you, but I don't believe it!"

He was just passing through; his connecting flight was leaving soon after mine. With only a few minutes to spend, we ducked into a coffee shop. I had not seen Barry since shortly after I retired. During training camp in Boston, Barry's leg and thumb had been injured. Because we roomed together, I knew all about it. Some question had arisen about the feasibility of suturing Barry's leg muscles, so nothing had been done. The doctors thought the sutures would not hold. The team management later released Barry from the team. Still unhealed, he had contacted an arbitration attorney, who had him examined by three non-partisan doctors. On their recommendation, his case was carried forward, seeking that year's salary. His attorney instructed him to find a witness who could testify to the time and extent of his injury. That is where I entered the picture. Barry called me in Memphis and asked if I remembered what happened.

"Of course I do," I assured him. "I'll be glad to testify." He offered to pay all the expenses of my trip to Minnesota for the arbitration hearing and told me when to meet him. I had not thought about my involvement in that hearing in years, but running into Barry in the Atlanta airport brought it all back. As we sat in the coffee shop trying to quickly bring each other up to date on ourselves, I shared with him how Jesus had changed my life.

He said, "Bull, I knew there was something different about you the minute I saw you. Do you remember the last time I saw you?"

"Hey, don't remind me. It wasn't exactly the kind of experience you try to remember. Seriously, Barry, I had not thought about all that stuff I got into in Minneapolis for a long time. Not until I saw you today."

I heard my flight announced, so we said our goodbyes and promised to stay in touch. My seat on the plane was next to a Christian young man with a briefcase full of paperwork, so after talking briefly, he took out his work and left me to my thoughts. Barry. Barry Brown. Seeing him had reminded me of the wild commotion I caused when I went to testify for him in Minneapolis.

As soon as I had met Barry at his hotel, I had suggested going out for "a few drinks." As the "few drinks" stacked up on the hotel bar tab and I showed no sign of stopping, Barry, thinking no doubt about the scheduled nine a.m. hearing, began insisting that we go to our room. I said, "No, you go on—I'm going out to look around this town."

After I had wandered in and out of a few joints getting drunker, I got into a ruckus with a black guy in a crowded bar. Others joined him, and the first thing I knew, I had five black guys fighting me. Three Indians sitting at the bar must have thought the odds were unfair because they got up and joined me. Chairs were flying through the air, people were trying to get out of our way, and we were slugging it out with anything we could pry loose. Someone called the cops, but before they got there, we had fought our way outside the building, where all the others scattered and ran.

I saw one of the black men run into a White Castle restaurant across the street. I went after him. The place was full of people, and the man I was chasing headed for a back door. I didn't think I could catch him, so I grabbed a wire basket on the counter and threw it at him. It missed him but hit a waitress, knocking her out. By then, I could hear sirens approaching, so I took off down an alley. I must have run up and down alleys for thirty minutes before the police got me, but when they caught me they took me to jail and locked me in a holding tank in solitary confinement. I asked them to call Barry, but they wouldn't talk to me.

I learned the next morning that they had called Barry at three o'clock and he had come down, but they would not allow him to see me. An assistant to his attorney came at seven a.m. to try to convince my captors to let me out for the arbitration hearing, but was told that I first had to satisfy court claims against me. Standing before the judge to answer charges, I was surprised to see the three Indians who had helped me fight the black guys the evening before. Apparently, they had gotten themselves into some other trouble. I didn't know what they had done, so I thought it might be best not to recognize them. After a brief glance in my direction, they showed no interest in renewing their acquaintance with me.

After the attorney got me out of there, at more expense to Barry, and after we had done all we could to make me presentable, we rushed to the hearing, arriving forty-five minutes late. In my foggy condition, I just wanted out of there, but one look at Barry's face jolted me into the reality of the position I had put him in. In the moments before I was sworn as a witness, I determined to concentrate on making Barry's injury as vivid as possible. The ruling came down in Barry's favor. He thanked me, and I flew back to Memphis.

Had I not bumped into him in Atlanta, much of what happened in Minneapolis would have remained forgotten.

As we parted after our time together in the airport, Barry grinned at me, shaking his head. "Bull," he said, "I'll never forget what you did; I can still see the way you looked when you showed up at that arbitration hearing. Man, my heart sank when I saw you. You were skinned up, scratched, bruised, both eyes were cut and glazed, one hand was bandaged, and you smelled like you had taken a bath in Jack Daniels. I've gotta' hand it to you though; you gave the performance of your life. The way you described my injury, I started hurting all over again." As we shook hands, he said, "Bull, some people say we don't have miracles today; well, I'm looking at one right now!"

I had only one answer to that. "Brother, you sure are! I'm just glad you can see it."

Soon after this, Dave Rowe, a thirteen-year football veteran, invited me to New York to give my testimony. Dave has since become a regional announcer for NFL games, but at that time was still playing ball. The San Diego Chargers were in New York for a game with the Jets. I knew I would be speaking to many of the men I had played football against. They all knew my former reputation.

After giving my testimony to the Chargers, I went to a chapel service for the Jets. As they listened to my story of how Jesus changed my life, several players decided to accept Him as Lord. The commitments made by men from both teams thrilled me because God was opening the doors and allowing me to see results from my witnessing.

Before I left New York, I told my old friend, Joe Namath, how God finally got my attention. I said, "Joe, the Lord has really blessed my life. Man, He changed me!"

Joe looked at me without saying a word.

"It's real," I said.

In deep sincerity, he replied, "Bramlett, I'm glad. If anybody ever needed it, you did."

"I'll go anywhere; I'll do everything I can to let people know what the Lord can do for them. I mean it, whatever it takes."

"I believe you. But you didn't have to tell me. It shows, Bull."

I'm sure some people didn't believe I was real at first. Some who had known me were probably curious to see the difference in the old Bramlett and the one who warned the lost about their sinful ways. Whatever the reason, I suddenly found myself swamped with invitations from all over the country to come and give my testimony. I had started out by telling how Jesus saved me and gave me a new life of peace and happiness, but as I gained experience, I began preaching my testimony. From the very beginning, I had given an opportunity everywhere I spoke for an on-the-spot decision.

By this time I was also in business with another man, selling air filters to industrial plants. Under the strain of an economic crunch, my partner got out of the business, leaving it with me. It became the Bramlett Industrial Supply Company, and if the profit had even come close to equaling the activity, it would have been a roaring success. Instead, it flopped.

Ron Young sold parts to me at a discount, but discounts are of little value when you are left holding the bag for payment of your product. I was a good salesman but a poor collector. Nancy was my secretary and bookkeeper, taking orders by phone. If she had to be away, she took the phone out into the yard with a pad and pencil so the boys could take the orders for her. Andy and Don had my company motto down to a fine art: IF YOU NEED IT, I'VE GOT IT . . . IF I DON'T HAVE IT, I'LL FIND IT . . . IF I CAN'T FIND IT, IT CAN'T BE FOUND.

Nancy and I have often laughed over our misfires with that business, though the pinch it put on us at that time was no laughing matter. When we finally realized that we could not collect enough of the money owed to us to keep our heads above water, we were deeply in debt to Ron Young.

Mr. Young offered me a job and agreed to let me pay him back by a systematic salary deduction. It took twelve years to pay that debt in full, but I believe God used those years to prepare me for full-time ministry. My position there kept me constantly in the company of other Christian men, and I saw every contact as an opportunity to witness to the saving grace of Jesus.

As I shared my faith with others, I listened. In church, I took notes on sermons as I sought to improve my own study of the Scriptures. One Sunday morning, Nancy was sick and I went to church without her. Brother Bobby Moore's message was titled "Turning The Corner." At his urging to be "sold out to God," totally surrendered without apology, the words of Romans 1:16 hit me with a powerful impact. During the invitation, I went down and knelt at the altar, weeping for my former life and all the years I had wasted. I committed myself to "turn the corner" with God. "I am not ashamed of the gospel of Christ: for it is the power of God unto salvation to every one that believeth . . ." these words became the declaration of my deepened commitment.

When I got home, I tried to explain my deepened commitment to Nancy. She must have thought, "Lord, what now? I wanted this man saved, but have you overdone it?" I was already publicly giving my testimony, witnessing to anyone who would listen, and passing out tracts everywhere I went. Now, here I was fired up to do more. I guess she could see herself and the boys sitting in a hut in Africa or in the jungles of Ecuador.

I didn't even take time to eat lunch. We had moved to a new neighborhood, so I took my Bible and went up and down our street knocking on doors, trying to tell the neighbors about Jesus. An elderly lady invited me in. I could see that her husband was irritated, but I was not going to be put off, so he got his hat and left. Having lived near me for awhile, I guess he'd seen nothing in me to give him reason to believe I had anything worthwhile to say. The lady and I sat down at the table in her kitchen and I explained the plan of salvation to her. We prayed together and she asked Jesus to come into her heart. Her response was just the gift of encouragement I needed. I later learned that the gift she received that day was far greater than my own satisfaction.

Unknown to me, that dear lady had been diagnosed as having throat cancer. Soon after my visit, she became bedridden, unable to speak. I thanked God that she didn't have to face her trials alone but could live her last days in the security of a Savior's love.

It was exciting to go to bed at night, wondering where God would take me the next day. In 1976, I participated in a campuswide series of activities at Carson-Newman College called "Celebrate '76." I saw it as a great opportunity to help young people who might be standing at a crossroads in their lives. I stayed in the boys' dormitory that weekend counseling young men to get serious about their choices for the future. As I attempted to guide them, little did I know the guidance God had in store for me.

Southerners are often accused of being racially prejudiced, especially against black people, but there's plenty of prejudice anywhere you go. At the time I grew up in Memphis, blacks and whites did not mingle socially, nor were they allowed to engage in sports activities together. If the cops saw us playing football together, they broke it up. The tackling was rough, often causing tempers to flare, and I am sure the cops stopped it as a precautionary measure against further trouble. By 1976, the races seemed to have adjusted well to each other on campus, and I was glad to see it working well at Carson-Newman.

Ken Sparks, then track coach and now head football coach of three former national championship teams, invited me to speak on campus at special services and in chapel. At the end of the chapel service, the crowded auditorium cleared quickly, leaving me alone at the front. As I stood there watching the students file out, I saw a tall young black man coming down the aisle toward me. He had long hair with colored beads braided into his hair, wearing the exact look that was a part of my prejudice. I looked around. Everyone else was gone, and this guy looked as if he had serious business on his mind. *Uh oh,* I thought, *what have I said now? This black dude is coming down here to whip me or I'm going to have to whip him. Lord, am I going to backslide right here?*

He walked up to me and said, "I didn't want to come here."

"You didn't?"

"No, I didn't."

"Well, why did you come then?" I asked him.

He just stood there biting his lip for a moment before speaking. I couldn't read his mood, so I waited for him to answer my question.

"Because coming to chapel is mandatory." Looking at me in a serious way, he added, "I'm real glad I came though."

"You are?" I still had not figured out what he had in mind.

"Yeah."

He seemed to be having a hard time getting it out. He told me his name was Clyde Smith. I asked him, "Clyde, why are you glad you came?"

He opened up a little then. "Mr. Bramlett, do you have a few minutes to talk to me? I want you to show me how I can meet your Jesus."

He was dead serious. "I've got plenty of time, Clyde. I'll show you what the Bible says about Jesus." We sat down together, and I shared with Clyde my Lord Jesus. After we talked and prayed together, he asked Christ to come into his heart and to take over his life.

How different this was to what I expected when Clyde had walked down the aisle to me. We were kneeling side by side, and when we looked up, I saw that Clyde's eyes were wet with tears. I knew mine were. We got up off our knees and for the first time in my life, I reached out and hugged a black man. We were both so happy because my Jesus was now Clyde Smith's Jesus, but there was more to it, much more, and we both knew it. The prejudices we had both carried all our lives had melted away in a few seconds in the presence of the One who loves a black man and a white man just the same.

Together, we had found the brotherhood that all men are meant to have in Christ, and we didn't ever want to lose it. Clyde was so grateful for the joy and peace that had come to him that he wanted to help his family and his friends to know his Jesus. I gave him a copy of *The Christian Life New Testament.*

Clyde was a freshman in college the year I met him at Carson-Newman. Upon his graduation, he began using his talents to work with young people. Today, Clyde Smith is a coach in Virginia and heads a Fellowship of Christian Athletes huddle group. I've thanked the Lord many times for using this young man to get it into Bull Bramlett's heart and head that the Spirit of God has no color—we have no racial barrier, only a Jesus barrier. When we confess Him in our hearts and serve Him with our lives, then, only then, will all our differences be resolved.

Prejudice is nothing more than a deep-seated resentment of those who are different from us, or who differ with us. Prejudice, resentment, and anger are all destructive forces in direct opposition to the Christian's growth. Absorbing the Word of God is the best defense against all negative forces—and I was constantly provided with occasions to prove it.

19

"All I Want for Christmas"

"Lord, there has to be some way you and I can work this thing out. I'm willing to do anything you want, if you'll just make little Stephen better. I love him so much, and I know you do, too. I have been thinking about giving up my Skoal, Lord; all you have to do is say the word and it's gone! If you will make that little boy better, I'll throw it away and never take another dip."

I was driving along, carrying on a one-sided conversation with God. I was concerned for a young victim of cystic fibrosis. In my business of selling industrial supplies, one of the places I called on was Ralston-Purina. The man I usually talked with there was Delbert. In my contacts, the first thing I did was tell about Jesus coming into my heart and giving me a new life. I started talking to Delbert. He wasn't interested in my spiritual experiences, but he listened. One day he told me that his son had cystic fibrosis and was often hospitalized for weeks. I asked if I could visit his son and Delbert gratefully consented.

I found Stephen to be a lovable little eight-year-old cottontop of incredible courage. He didn't talk much, but he loved to listen to my stories. We played games together. Visiting Stephen every week became a habit. I think I was giving time to him at first because I felt guilty for neglecting my boys in the first years of their lives, but I soon grew to love the little guy so much I looked forward to being with him.

He had improved and was out of the hospital when I had what I thought was a good idea. I wanted to see Stephen, so I asked Ron Young to go with me to the home. I had had no success convinc-

ing Delbert to become a Christian, so I wanted Ron to give it a
try. While he witnessed to Delbert, I could visit with Stephen.

Soon after we arrived, I left to play with Stephen and his older
brother and sister, leaving Ron a clear field with Delbert. I had a
great time with the three kids, explaining to them what it means
to be a Christian. Before I left, all three prayed with me for Jesus
to be their Savior. Delbert was not of a mind to do that. He let
Ron talk but resisted making a decision.

My concern for Stephen was so deep that I talked to others
about him, asking them to pray for him and visit him. Justin
Canale, a former Patriots teammate from Memphis, became interested and took some of the World Football League players to the
hospital to see Stephen. I went to see him once or twice a week,
and when I was in the car alone I was usually trying to make a
deal with God for Stephen to get better. I said, "Lord, I don't
drink, I'm not running around—this snuff isn't hurting anyone,
but I'll even give that up." I guess the Lord must have gotten
pretty sick of that because one day he stopped me cold. He made
me look at myself. I didn't like what I saw.

I had used snuff since I was a kid swiping it out of my grandparents' Garrett Snuff jars. In college, I changed to Skoal and
Copenhagen. The habit got such a hold on me that I saw it as a
necessity like food or drink. I kept a fancy spittoon at home,
carrying a more modest receptacle (a can) in my car. Whenever I
got out of the car to talk to someone about Jesus, I'd spit my snuff
out before I witnessed, then afterward, get another dip and go on
down the road. It had never occurred to me that I was a stum-
bling block in my own home; my boys tried to imitate everything
I did.

When Andy was seven years old, I was sitting in the living
room with a big dip of Skoal and he asked for some. I filled his
lower lip with it and went back to reading my newspaper. A few
minutes later, I heard Don say, "You look funny," and I looked
up to see Andy swaying on his feet. He was as white as a ghost.
He suddenly began throwing up all over me. He was so sick his
eyes were glazed. I sent him to the bathroom and as he staggered
down the hall, I said, "Run water in the tub and get in it."

After all the mess was cleaned up, we realized that Andy had been gone for a long time. We went looking for him and when we got to the bathroom, he was lying stretched out in the dry tub, completely naked. The poor little guy was so sick, he didn't know what he was doing. It was a good thing he hadn't turned the water on. He might have drowned.

As I drove along that day talking to the Lord about Stephen, that incident with Andy came clearly to my mind, and I suddenly realized what the Spirit of God was saying to me: "John, when I make deals, I issue the conditions, not you! Your position is to trust me—and obey me. Little Stephen is Mine and because he is, he'll receive the best." In the revelation of that moment, I saw my snuff-dipping as a spiritual barrier to my effectiveness as a witness. I rolled down the window and threw out the snuff and my can.

Stephen was spending more and more time in the hospital. His condition worsened, but he was still able to enjoy my visits. I was especially busy one week and didn't go to see him. I finally got some free time that Saturday afternoon, and I called his mother. She told me that he had felt better all day, had several visitors, and things were going well. I told her I would see them the following day.

After dinner, I felt suddenly impressed to go to the hospital. As I walked down the hall of the hospital to Stephen's room, I met his mother. She seemed agitated, and before I could speak, she said, "John, I'm so glad you are here."

"What's wrong?" I asked.

"After you called, Stephen suddenly took a turn for the worse. His breathing is getting harder, and he is very uncomfortable. So far, nothing they have done has helped . . . ."

"Where is Delbert?" I could see that she needed him.

"I don't know," she said.

I had an idea where I might find him. Delbert drank in the same places I had once hung out in, and I knew them all. As reassuringly as I could, I said, "Look—don't worry. I'm going in to see Stephen for just a minute, then I'll go find his dad."

I went into the room and sat down on the side of the bed.

Stephen rolled over and his little face lit up. He said, "John, do you know who was here a little while ago?"

"No, who?" I asked.

Looking straight into my eyes, he said, "Jesus! He sat down on my bed and He touched my side. He made me feel better, John."

I couldn't speak. He smiled and said, "I'm going to roll over on my side and maybe He will touch that side and make it feel better."

After he rolled over, he said, "John, you know God made the moon and the stars, and the sun . . . and He made you and me, and Mama and Daddy, and everybody." He reached out and touched my hand, and said, "You know, John, if it weren't for God, there would be *nothing.*"

This, from an eight-year-old boy who had never been able to go to church, who had known the Lord for only a few months, was overwhelming. I listened as he spoke of the things he had read in the New Testament I had given him. He said, "I had a dream, John; it was about a snake, and he was trying to get me. But there was a big rock, and it killed that snake." In amazement, I thought, that is a clear picture of Satan and Jesus, the Rock.

When he drifted off to sleep, I told his mother, "I'm going to find his dad. I'll be back soon."

On the way to my car, I saw Delbert coming across the parking lot with a six-pack of beer in one hand and an open can in the other. I met him, and said, "Man, your boy needs you to come on up and see him. He isn't doing well, and he wants to talk to you."

When we got to the bed, Stephen reached up and caught Delbert's arm. He said, "Daddy, did you know God made everything and everybody? He made the sun and stars; He made you and Mama, and me—and John. And Daddy—"he hesitated, then said, "Daddy, I'm going to Heaven, and . . . Daddy, I want you to go to Heaven. Will you, Daddy? Will you go to Heaven and be with me?"

Delbert immediately answered, "Yeah, son, I'll go to Heaven with you." He motioned for me to follow him outside. In the hall, he grabbed me by the collar and demanded, "What have you been telling my boy? I want to know what kind of stuff you are putting in his head!"

"I haven't been putting anything into his head. I have told him about Jesus, and the night Ron Young and I came to your home, your son gave his life to Christ."

Delbert's wife came out in the hall. She reached out and took his hand off my collar, and we all went back inside. I thought I should leave, but when I stood to go, Delbert said, "No, John, I don't want you to go. Please stay." I sat back down.

We sat beside Stephen's bed all night. He awakened from time to time to describe scenes of beauty he was seeing. Once he roused to say to his mother, "Mama, look at me; Mama, ain't I pretty?" Time passed and again he woke and cried out, "Mama, Mama, look at the peach trees . . . and the apple trees! Ain't they pretty?" Not long afterward, he opened his eyes and spoke directly to me. "John, tomorrow . . . tomorrow, after the sun comes up, Jesus is going to make me better." They were the last words he spoke.

I sat there thinking of my flawed image of God in my foolish attempt to bargain with Him to make Stephen better. What an insult to Almighty God, to suggest that some feeble favor from me could determine His concern for another of His children.

I was sitting on the side of the bed when daylight came. Stephen was still sleeping fitfully. I watched as the first rays of morning sun streamed in through the window. Little Stephen suddenly bolted upright on his feet in the bed, stretching his arms straight up over his head. Just as quickly, he fell back down. I caught him in my arms as he fell, and Jesus made him better. Stephen had gone home to be with Jesus for Eternity.

"Precious in the sight of the LORD is the death of his saints."[1]

I felt a deep sense of loss and grief, but I knew I had gained something very precious from my relationship with this little boy. My faith was strengthened through this experience. As Nancy and I talked it over at home, we thanked God for giving that little boy with no hope of a better physical life, a matchless joy in his hope of a beautiful life in Heaven. We opened our Bible and read together 2 Corinthians 5:8: "We are confident, I say, and willing rather to be absent from the body, and to be present with the Lord."

Delbert asked me to speak at his son's funeral. It was tough. Our lives had become intertwined. I told the people the simple story of Stephen's commitment to Christ and shared the glimpse of Heaven he had given us during his last night on earth.

Through all that happened, and in the years following, inasmuch as I know, Stephen's father never made a profession of faith in the Lord. As the result of an accident, he lay in a coma for two years before he died. I visited him many times in the hospital, reading the Bible to him each time and praying for him. He just lay there with his eyes open; I wondered if he could hear the words I spoke.

When Nancy and I made Christ the center of our home, we began teaching Andy and Don the love of Jesus. We wanted them to know Him in the fullness we knew Him. Realizing at last the importance of Christian living within the home, we wanted every child to have it. Remembering how I had failed my family caused me to give special attention to activities aimed at helping children to grow spiritually. For years I had played Santa Claus at Christmas. Before I met Christ, I was dressing up in the red suit and going into homes on Christmas Eve, giving candy and fruit to kids—along with a lot of "bull" I'm sure, because I was usually drunk. After I was saved, I thought about what a travesty I had made of this sacred holiday all of my adult life, drinking to celebrate Jesus' birthday.

I couldn't wait for my first Christmas with Jesus, so I began the celebration a month early. I hoped somehow to wipe out of my family's mind all those times I had ruined it for them. We decorated, we talked about the birth of Jesus, we sang carols, we did it all! Nancy and the boys loved it.

When Christmas Eve finally came, I put on the Santa Claus suit and went out to some of the same places I had gone before, but this was a different Santa. This one had a mission. When children sat on my lap to tell what they wanted, I told them about Jesus. I gave their parents gospel tracts. I talked to fathers about taking their children to church, not just sending them. Andy and Don caught the true spirit of giving and began sharing their Christian faith along with their gift-giving. They learned to do it by helping me distribute gifts to those in need when they were still young; they do it now as young men because it has become important to them to share with others the joy of what Jesus has done in their own family.

I had known the Lord for almost three years when something happened that proved to me how impressionable those early childhood years are. I came home from work one day about a week before Christmas and found a letter in the mailbox addressed to me. It was from Don's teacher. Before I finished reading it, tears were streaming down my face. I knew I had to find some way to share this with others. I called a newspaper reporter and told him about it. After hearing it, he said, "Man, let me write that down. Yes, we need to get that in the paper."

On Christmas Eve, the *Memphis Press-Scimitar* ran this story:

Christmas isn't until tomorrow, but John Bramlett, the former Memphis State and All-Pro linebacker, says no present he'll receive tomorrow will be as heart warming as the one he got last week from a teacher at Towering Oaks School where his son, Don, fourteen, is in the eighth grade. The teacher, Mrs. Anita Blankenship, assigned Don's class a project of writing a paragraph on the theme, "All I Want For Christmas Is . . . ." Mrs. Blankenship was so touched by Don's paragraph that she sent it to Bramlett as an early Christmas present.

The paragraph that Don had written, follows:

All I Won't for Christmas cls.

All I want for Christmas is for my family and I to have a very merry Christmas, like the other two Christmases we've had. My dad was out drinking and fighting three years ago and we were all worrying about him and wondering when he will come back while opening our presents, it was so miserable through those years. Now we have a happy and merry Christmas, after he accepted Jesus in his heart and we have a lot to be thankful for. This is all I want for Christmas and I got it.

When the paper came, Nancy and I read it together. Our son's past misery and present joy were all there in that little paragraph, but something else was there: his thankfulness to God who had made the joy possible.

I loved my boys before I became a Christian, but had I cared for them in the right way, I would have seen that the way I lived was a blueprint for teaching them a shortcut to Hell. In their love for me, they imitated everything I did. As young boys, they looked forward to getting old enough to go out drinking with me. Before that could happen, God changed me. When Nancy and I joined a church, the boys went with us. I had explained as clearly as I could how Jesus saved me, and both Andy and Don wanted to believe they were somehow included. It took two years for me to see that as simple as the act of accepting Jesus is, the working of the Holy Spirit is unfathomable. I try to help others understand what they must do to know God. After that, it becomes a personal matter. When Jesus knocks, the person behind the door is the only one who can lift the latch.

Andy went to a youth camp from Central Church, and on the evening he returned, at bedtime, he came and got on the bed with me. He said, "Dad, I've got something to tell you."

"Sure, how was your trip?"

"It was good," he answered, "but there is something I need to tell you about it. Something happened."

"Really?" I asked. "Well, let's hear it."

He hesitated. "I don't know what you're going to think; but I gave my life to Christ."

It surprised me, but I just said quietly, "Son, I want to hear all about it."

He told me then how happy he was after I changed; how he believed that if he could be just like me, he could help to make it last. He said, "Dad, I know you thought I was a Christian, but I wasn't. At camp, I heard Milton Hatcher preach on Hell, and I knew if I died right then, that's where I'd go. I don't want to go to Hell. I want to go to Heaven, so I trusted Christ."

"So how is it now? Are you okay, Son?"

"It's all different, Dad. I know I belong to Jesus. I just know."

Andy stopped talking and started crying. I was glad to see his tears because mine were already running down my face. Nancy walked in and at the sight of us, she started crying too. When Andy had gone forward with us for church membership, his desire was for the fringe benefits—in his case, the joy of a Christian home. And true to His promise to honor those who honor Him, God blessed that. For two years, He watched over Andy until He brought him to Fall Creek Falls camp to hear Milton Hatcher describe Hell. Andy said something afterward that really spoke to my heart. He said, "I read my Bible all the way from Cookeville

to Memphis on the way home from camp." A fourteen-year-old
boy finding in the Word of God something to hold his interest for
several hours was proof to me that neither age, occupation, nor
education can limit God's ability to communicate with those who
love Him.

Andy played football in high school and upon graduation, he
received a scholarship to Carson-Newman College. He went to
the University of Tennessee at Martin his second year, then came
home to Memphis State University, graduating from there. In his
last years of college, Andy was gaining maturity; he began accepting invitations to speak to school assemblies and banquets,
and I began to wonder if God was steering him toward becoming
a preacher.

Andy had spoken in Ingram Boulevard Church when the pastor, Dr. Bob Wiggins, approached him about accepting a position
as Interim Youth Pastor. Andy was still in school and playing ball,
so after thinking it through and praying about it, he decided he
could give it the time required. He liked the work, especially the
thrill of filling the pulpit when the pastor was away. He felt
pulled in the direction of the ministry but he wanted to be sure. I
wanted him to be sure too. I told him, "Son, there are lots of
preachers, and some of them, God didn't call. It may be the only
job in the world you can fail at while giving it your best, but that
is what will happen if God hasn't called you." He agreed.

"Dad, why don't I just leave the doors open? I'm graduating
in two weeks. I'll send out resumes and start going on job interviews. I'll let the Lord decide. If He wants me to go into the
ministry, I won't be offered a job. If He wants me somewhere
else, He will show me."

After several interviews, nothing happened. Then he got a call
from a pharmaceutical company, offering him a job. It had been
his dream all along to become a professional medical representa-
tive, but he had pushed it to the back of his mind, trying to be
objective about his future.

A few days later, he told Nancy and me, "I hope you aren't
disappointed. You both know, if there is a place where God needs

people more than any other, it is in the business world. I believe that is where He wants me."

I was convinced. Andy is just as excited today about his work as he was then. As he shares some of his experiences of witnessing to lost people, I am thankful that he was willing to leave his vocational decision to the one who could underwrite it.

Through my sons, I've come to understand what a father means to a boy. A boy loves his mother, but he lives for his father. His strongest desire is to have his dad's approval and love. A boy who grows up with the assurance of his father's love and affection is already halfway home before he starts. I know the hunger a boy feels in his heart for that assurance, and I thank God today that in all those years I served the devil, my boys believed in my love for them. Our relationship has helped me to accept those impossible-to-understand things in my own father—and to wash away any dregs of bitterness.

At MSU our boys became close friends with a fine Christian boy, Geddes Self III, and Jack Oliver, who were suitemates in the athletic dorm. The four boys roomed together, and during that time Jack committed his life to Christ. After graduation Geddes married, but Jack, who had become like a third son to Nancy and me, wanted to play ball.

Jack loved sports and had become a fine football player. During the 1987 football players' strike, he played for the Chicago Bears in the three replacement games.

At the beginning of the same season, Don went as a free agent to the Minnesota Vikings. Leaving home, he said, "Dad, I'll give it my best shot." I feel certain he did, but he was released before the strike. When the regulars went out on strike, the Tampa Bay Buccaneers called Don. He had been there for only one week when the Vikings called and asked him to come back, so Don played the replacement games for Minnesota.

All three are now out of school, out of football, and into jobs they enjoy. Andy bought a house, and all three moved into it. They claim to value their privacy, but I haven't heard of them turning down any dinner invitations from Nancy. As I rake them

over the coals about anything that comes to my mind, kidding
them, threatening to change the locks on our house, I sit at the
table with them and ask in my heart what I could possibly ever do
to repay even a little the gift that God laid on "Bull" Bramlett in
these three young men.

Looking back on our boys' childhood, Nancy and I can see
ways in which the Lord was growing us up together. I didn't
discipline my boys until I became a Christian. When I read,
"Foolishness is bound in the heart of a child; but the rod of
correction shall drive it far from him,"[2] I started cracking down
on them. I was afraid that left to themselves, bad habits would
form patterns too strong to break.

One day Nancy and I had been away from home for several
hours and when we came in, Andy and Don were sitting quietly
on the sofa with their hands folded on their laps. This was so
abnormal, we immediately asked, "What's wrong here? What
happened?"

Andy nudged Don with his elbow. "Tell them."

"No, you tell them," Don said.

I said, "Look, I don't care who tells it, but one of you better
start talking . . . now!"

Soon after we had left the house, they had gotten into an argument. As it heated up, Don took off after Andy with a golf club.
Andy ran through the house into his room and locked the door.
Don threw the golf club and it went all the way through the door,
knocking a hole as big as your fist. That solved the problem of
whatever they were mad at each other about, because now they
had a bigger problem: Daddy.

They put their heads together and quickly came up with what
they thought was a perfect solution—replace the door before we
got home. The people across the street had recently moved out,
so they gathered up screw drivers and hammers and went over to
the vacant house to find a door they could take off. They got their
door, but it didn't fit Andy's doorway. Not ready to give up, they
took off down the street to their grandparents' house. Ad helped
them check out her doors, but none of them would fit. By then it

was time for Nancy and me to get home, so they were forced to tell us their story.

After I had all the facts, I asked, "Boys, you knew better, didn't you?"

"Yes, sir," they mumbled.

"Come with me," I said, leading the way to the back bedroom.

I got my big paddle out of the closet. "You've done wrong," I said, "and you know you have to be punished. Both of you know how to behave. I think a good whipping with this paddle will help you to remember this."

Their eyes were on their feet. I said, "Boys, I love you and I don't want to whip you, but when you do wrong someone has to pay the penalty. I am going to take your whipping for you." Their eyes snapped up.

I said, "Come here, Andy." I gave him the paddle, turned my back, and bent over. "Now, lay it on me. Come on, either you'll do this right, or I'll whip you!" At first he couldn't do it, but as I urged him on, he began to put his heart into it. That big paddle brought tears to my eyes.

When he put it down, Don knew he was next. He couldn't pick up the paddle. He began to cry. "No, Daddy, please don't make me do it! I can't hit you, Daddy! I love you too much, Daddy, please don't make me . . . ." He was crying so hard I felt mean about insisting, but I made him hit me a few licks. That was the worst punishment Don could have had; he is so tenderhearted that the thought of inflicting pain on me was more than he could handle.

Soon after the boys were saved, they began inviting their friends into our home for Bible study. As time passed, we had so many young people coming, our living room was too small to accommodate them. We just got rid of a wall and opened up two rooms into one. Ken Whitten taught our group, a group that grew to 110 people.

I believe the Word of God teaches that we need balance in Christianity even more than in football—and *I know* what is going to happen when a team lacking a balanced offense or defense goes on the field. If a team expects to win, every man must master his position. Every Christian needs Bible knowledge, a desire to know Jesus better, and the common sense to help people where they are hurting.

People sometimes talk about faith as if God sits up there passing it out at random. "Faith cometh by hearing, and hearing by the word of God."[3] If we hear something, really *hear* it, we're already on our way to doing something about it. I've tried to show my boys that you can't stand back waiting for someone to throw you the ball—you've got to get open and be ready for it.

20

The Power in a Tamed Bull

It was a great day for golf, with high skies and a soft breeze, but I was out on the course with something more urgent in mind: fishing. I had been witnessing to my neighbor, Frank Snyder, but somehow he always managed to slip off the hook.

Frank, a fine six-foot-seven athlete who had played basketball in college, had been two years ahead of me at Memphis State. He had joined the Marines out of high school, starting college after he came out of the service. After he graduated, I didn't see him again until I moved across the street from him. Before I became a Christian, we had played poker together, always with a few drinks. Frank had not lived the rough life I had, so he probably thought that if it took something that drastic to bring me into line, it was a good thing for me—but he didn't need it.

That day on the golf course, I brought up the subject soon after we started playing. "Frank, if you'll commit your life to Christ, you've no idea what He can do for you."

We stopped in the shade of a tree as Frank very seriously explained how he felt. "John, I know you think because this works for you, I need it too. I can see how you really needed it. Man, you were mean! This religion is what you needed to get your life together. It's different for me—I don't do the things you did."

I tried to explain that even the finest moral character won't save a person. "Frank, I understand that you are a good man. My wife was a good person, really good! But when she began studying the Bible she saw that being morally good is not enough. Being 'good' is trying to do it all on your own. We have to believe in Jesus Christ."

"Well, John, I just don't see it the same way you do. I may drink a beer occasionally, but John, I'm all right."

Frank was not the kind of man to get upset if he didn't agree with you, so whenever we saw each other after that, I felt free to go on witnessing to him, and he didn't mind putting me off.

Frank got sick and grew steadily worse. He was diagnosed as having a brain tumor and was in and out of the hospital for several months. I went by the hospital to visit with him as often as I could. I was praying for him, and for his nice wife and daughter, who were having a tough time accepting his condition.

Talking with Jimmy Burell one day and reminiscing about all the times he had helped me out financially when I first became a Christian, I mentioned Frank's illness. I saw that I had struck a nerve. "My goodness, John, I've got a friend who is in the same boat, fighting cancer. The doctors have told him that he just has a few months to live. The big difference is, my friend knows the Lord."

I was so concerned about Frank, I suggested, "Jimmy, why don't you take your friend to see Frank? Maybe he can share some of what he is going through and help Frank."

He agreed. They went to see Frank. I'm sure he appreciated their effort to help him, but he still saw no need to change.

A few weeks later, I was having my quiet time early one morning. I had developed the habit of getting up to have some time alone before going to work. Nancy never interrupted my prayer times; if someone called early, she usually took their number so I could call them back. But on this particular morning, she came to the door and said, "Honey, I hate to bother you, but I think you ought to come to the phone now. Frank Snyder wants to talk to you."

The first words he spoke went straight to my heart. "John, I know it's early, but I couldn't wait to tell you. John, I want you to be the first to know what just happened. When I woke up this morning, I got out of bed, I got down on my knees and gave my heart to the Lord Jesus Christ. He is my personal Lord and Savior this morning, John."

I can't express strongly enough the relief I felt that God had finally gotten through to Frank Snyder, a good man but lost without Christ. Just a few short weeks later, Frank went home to be with Jesus.

As I thanked and praised God for saving Frank and for letting me know, I reflected on how often I seemed to cross paths with people who were familiar with my old lifestyle. After God changed me, the one thing that kept me from 100 percent happiness was an occasional nagging reminder of someone I had hurt in the past. I apologized to those I could, but when the response was unforgiving, it really grieved me. Then God demonstrated to me that my sin was against Him, and what He forgave me, He could also make right with the ones I had wronged.

A week before I was to preach a revival in a Memphis church, the pastor went out into the community inviting people to come and hear me speak. He mentioned to one man that I had played football. That got the man's attention.

"Wait a minute," he said. "This man—did he play football at Memphis State?"

"Yes, he did," the minister answered.

"And did he play pro football too?"

"Yes."

"Are you sure his name is John Bramlett?"

"Yes."

The pastor later described to me the look of amazement that came over the man's face as he said, "Man, there is no way this could be the same John Bramlett I know. There is no way that man could ever be a Christian." He then told the preacher how he came to know John Bramlett.

"Man," he said, "I was in Methodist Hospital, really sick. This Memphis State football player had hit someone head to head in a game and jammed his neck. The doctors put him in traction in the room with me. One evening after visiting hours, a man came in there and helped him get out of traction. He got out of bed in his pajamas, put on some house shoes and a robe, and the two of them took off. I don't know where they went; I didn't care where they went."

The man stopped, shook his head as if he still found it hard to believe, then continued. "I know this—he almost killed me. At three in the morning, those two men came back to that room where I was lying in a deep sleep with my mouth open. This crazy man, John Bramlett, took a can of beer and started pouring it in my mouth. The first thing I knew I was choking and struggling to breathe. I was puking and heaving—it was awful! I actually thought I was dying, and there were these two lunatics laughing their heads off! Nurses and orderlies were working over me, trying to keep me alive, which they did. But it was an ordeal I've never forgot!"

He promised the pastor he would come to the revival. "I wouldn't miss it," he said. "If that man is the same John Bramlett I know, I'll recognize him. Don't worry, I'll be there!"

The pastor had not shared this conversation with me, but as I preached the Word at the revival, I felt moved to tell experiences from my past before I knew the Lord and to describe again how Jesus came into my heart and made me a new man.

In closing, I walked up and down the aisles asking the congregation, "Do you know the Lord? Is He real to you today?" The man who knew me from the hospital was next to the aisle. With no idea who he was, I asked, "Sir, are you saved?"

Looking into my eyes, he said, "No. I'm not. But I would like to be."

A strong feeling of closeness with this man came over me. As he took my outstretched hand, he said, "John, if God can save a man like you, I know he can save a man like me."

The man received Jesus in his heart that day and after the service was over, he stayed to talk with me. He and the pastor told me about their conversation, and I began to remember what happened that night when I was just a college boy.

Larry Sutton was the friend who came to Methodist Hospital and helped me slip past the nurses' station and out to the car. We had gone to Hernando's Hideaway in Memphis, where we danced and drank until three in the morning. It was easy at that hour to sneak back in the room, carrying our beer. Seeing that poor, sick man lying there with his mouth open, snoring, struck me in my drunken state as funny. I didn't even think of the effect pouring that beer down his throat could have on him. In recent years Larry became a Christian, thereby creating an even stronger bond between us. Today we find our past escapades hard to believe.

As my new-found friend and I talked, it thrilled my heart to see how God's grace had protected us both, keeping me from the consequences of my thoughtless act and sparing him for this day. He had nothing but compassion for me. "And be ye kind one to another, tenderhearted, forgiving one another, even as God for Christ's sake hath forgiven you."[1]

I thought of Mr. Everitt's kindness to me during the years I played baseball for him. I felt a sudden urge to let him see how God had changed me. I think I wanted him to know that his hope that I would amount to something was at least somewhat realized. I went to see him. We had a long talk about God's providential care through all the trouble I'd brought on myself.

As I tried to explain to him how real Jesus was to me, I started to cry. Mr. Everitt broke down too. He was one of those good men who practiced fair play with everyone, but he had lived all his life without knowing Jesus. As we talked he became excited about the power of God to change a life. He believed God was able because he knew how I had lived before I met Jesus.

Mr. Everitt made a commitment to follow the Lord that day. Soon he started going to church regularly, and at ninety-three, that old fellow who had given so many boys a chance to develop athletic talents, decided to be baptized. Several of the men who had played baseball for him came to his church to be with him for his baptismal service.

One of my friends, Jack Hoelscher, later told me how happy Mr. Everitt was as he served the Lord in the last years of his life. "He couldn't stop talking about what Christ had done for him. He loved the Bible, and it was so exciting to him."

Jack chuckled. "One reason I hated to call him or go to see him, John—I knew I was going to have to listen while he told me all about you. He was so proud of you. I don't know how many times he told me about you leading him to the Lord."

Another person who knew how wild I'd been was Milton

Hatcher. Long before he became a Christian and preached the sermon that convinced Andy of the reality of hell, Milton's barber shop was a popular hangout for high school boys. When I was in Humes High, I got my flat-top haircuts from him, and he shared his whiskey with me.

In 1964 Milton met Jesus, and the impact left him with a deep desire to help people, especially those with drinking problems or who were just down and out. He secured a building in Memphis and opened the Calvary Rescue Mission. He provided food, clean clothes, and a bed for those who came. All he asked in exchange was the opportunity to share the message that Jesus could solve their problems permanently.

After I became a Christian, I'd go by the mission to talk with Milton. One day I had an idea. "Milton, you've got the perfect setup here for witnessing to people, and not just the ones who *know* they're needy. Why don't we start a men's luncheon? One day each week we'll invite businessmen to come and eat lunch, then go to the chapel for a time of music and testimony. This would be a chance to invite men, not to an organization or a church—but to Jesus!"

He was excited about it. "I'll have the food ready," he promised. "You just take care of the chapel service."

I agreed, and since we began the men's luncheons, I've led singing, preached on occasion, and witnessed to a number of people one on one. In turn, the businessmen have responded generously. They have roofed the building, bought fans, and improved the bathroom facilities.

Of all those from my past whom God has brought back into my life, George Atkinson has most influenced my being in a full-time ministry without the distractions of trying to make a living. God used George to open the door to the ministry I am now in.

I first met George when I was making an all-out effort to gain enough weight and brawn to try out for the Denver Broncos. Allen Hurst sent me a weight-lifting program designed to develop muscular strength, and the only convenient place with the right facilities was the Mason Y.M.C.A.

Right after I started going to the Y, I singled out George Atkinson to rag because he was a rabid supporter of my college football rival, "Ole Miss." He was a heavy-set man, easygoing, but with a gruff voice and manner. As soon as the stretching exercises began, I would start the kidding and never let up. "Come on, Fat Man," I'd yell, "get those legs up." Or "Reach for it, 'Ole Miss,' you can do it!"

After I became a Christian and went to work for Ron Young, I used to call on Planters Gin Company. I was driving an old, beat-up car that Joe Cooper had given me from his used car lot on Bellevue, and while I was at the gin company one day, George, one of the company owners, came outside and looked at my car. I knew my tires were worn slick, but I didn't have money for new ones.

George liked to get on my case, so in his loud, hoarse voice, he said, "Bramlett, do you mean to tell me you go around telling people about Jesus, looking like this? You ought to straighten up, get some rubber on those wheels!"

I answered, "Yeah, that's right, George. When the Lord blesses me and I get some money, I'm going to get some new tires."

He laughed. "Well, the Lord has just blessed you, Boy—go get you some wheels." He paid for a new set of tires for my car.

Sometime later George suffered a stroke. He was in intensive care, and couldn't talk, but I went by the hospital each week to visit with his family. Sometimes I'd see his daughter and son-in-law there.

One day when I got there, I found George's daughter and her husband alone in the waiting room. I asked them if they knew the Lord, and they became convinced of their need. Before we parted, both prayed to receive Jesus.

George's dream was that his daughter and her husband would become Christians. After George died, a mutual friend told me, "I don't know if anyone ever told you, John, but before George died, he got to see this come true. His daughter and son-in-law told him one day that they had committed their lives to Christ. I wanted you to know that you had a hand in the greatest gift George could have received. They told George that you were the one who led them to the Lord."

Soon after George's death, his brother, E. W., called me and asked me to come over to the cotton gin company. When I got there, he said, "John, you and George argued, laughed, and joked—but old George really loved you. He always wanted to help you. He believed in what you were doing. He and I have talked about how you give up your time at night and on weekends to go and carry the gospel, and we know you are real."

"I appreciate that, E. W.," I said, "and I know how George felt. He was continually after me to start my own ministry, but I'm already doing all I can. I don't turn anyone down."

E. W. said, "John, just listen to me. George always wanted a part in what you were doing. Now, if you could give all your time to ministering, have you thought of what you would be able to do? Think about it, John!" Allowing that to soak in for a moment, he asked, "John, why don't we start the John Bramlett Ministry in honor of George? Would you do that?"

I didn't see how I could argue. "Okay," I said, "I'll do that." Businessmen who knew I was already involved around the clock in spreading the gospel agreed to give money to buy gas, tracts, and Bibles. It never amounted to more than $3,000 a year, but it was a tremendous boost for me. It was carried on quietly, without any publicity, for almost ten years. I continued to work; I was still paying Ron Young the debt that I had incurred when my own small business failed.

In 1985, when the debt was paid in full, I felt free to resign my job with Ron and go all out in the ministry. The same four dedicated Christian men who formed my first Board of Directors still serve today. Ken Meador, one of the two men who witnessed to me of Christ's love that night in my home in 1973, is the president. E. W. Atkinson, Sr. (George's brother), and Charlie Brand are co-vice presidents, and E. W. Atkinson, Jr., is the treasurer. Since then, we have added lawyer, Bruce Brooke, as secretary.

At a Bible study breakfast, a man I didn't know felt led to give me $1,000 to make a down payment on a Datsun station wagon to replace the battered old junk heap I was driving. After five years and 150,000 miles on the station wagon, Jesse McClerkin, a car dealer, came to our house and took it away. In its place in the driveway, he left a brand new Datsun on which I put 100,000 miles. God always seems to send someone at just the right time.

Even as He sends others to our rescue, I believe the Lord is using us in His timely rescue of others. I was speaking at a junior high school football banquet in Memphis where my boys were involved in school sports when I first became aware of Paul Kuhlman's pain.

Paul and his wife, Judy, had three sons who were friends with my sons. Judy and Nancy were friends. I somehow got the impression as I spoke at the banquet that night that Paul, who seemed to enjoy the part of my speech that dealt with pro sports, lost much of his enthusiasm as I began to work my Christian testimony into the closing moments. As I asked for those who were there without Christ to invite Him into their hearts as we bowed our heads for prayer, I caught a look of disapproval on Paul Kuhlman's face. He did not bow his head. Long after we became friends, he admitted the antagonism he had felt during that prayer.

A house in the Kuhlman's neighborhood came on the market, and Nancy and I bought it. I doubt that Paul planned to promote a relationship with me, but it just seemed to happen that we were often together. One would have to realize my incompetence at repairing things to appreciate Nancy's method of handling the mechanical problems that develop at our house.

The first time I came in to find Paul and Judy Kuhlman helping Nancy fix the toilet, I realized what a great opportunity God had given me to find out where Paul stood spiritually. He was quick to let me know that whatever I thought I had, he didn't need it. He was a congenial fellow, very accommodating and uncommonly skilled at fixing everything around the house. All the time he was caulking windows, hanging blinds, and opening drainpipes, I was telling him how the love of Jesus had transformed my life. I was careful not to push him too far, but I kept contact with him.

I continued to pray for him, and I witnessed to him every chance I got, but I was not seeing much progress. During the Christmas season I could see that Paul drank heavily. Business was not flourishing for him, and his marriage was in trouble. His sons were drifting away from him. He confessed later that during the holidays, he felt so alienated from his family that he decided as a last resort to attend Sunday evening church service with them.

The next morning was cold and clear with about a foot of snow on the ground. Nancy and I were having coffee when the doorbell rang. When I opened the door, Paul and Judy were standing there. Before I could speak, Paul's eyes met mine, and I saw tears spill over and run down his cheeks. They didn't need to explain; his face and the look in his eyes told the story for me, for I had once stood where he was standing.

The four of us cried together and hugged each other. Paul finally said, "John, I got saved last night."

As I put a Bible in his hands, I told him, "This is the beginning of a life you'll never regret. But the next step is so important, you can't afford to put it off. We need to get you started studying the Word."

It was exciting to hear Paul tell how the Spirit of God spoke to him as he sat in church with his family the night before. As the minister preached the love of Jesus, Paul had suddenly begun putting it together with the experiences I had been sharing with him. He said, "It was just like raising a window shade to let the light in. I knew I should go forward for prayer, but I let my pride take over. I didn't feel that I could admit in front of all those people that I was a sinner. I guess you could say I was petrified in the pew."

After he and Judy returned home, though, the crisis came to a head. Judy suggested that they live apart for awhile in order to think objectively about their marriage. She had no idea of the turmoil within Paul; she just felt that she could no longer live in the negative atmosphere of their present marriage.

After she went to bed, Paul sat alone looking at the dismal prospect of his future. In desperation, he fell to his knees and asked Jesus to save him. Reflecting on that night, he said, "I didn't even know who He was, but something told me that He was the only hope I had."

Paul spent the entire evening in prayer, asking God to forgive him all the transgressions, all the wrong choices, of his life. When Judy entered the kitchen the next morning, he was there waiting for her. His first words convinced her that their life together was about to change.

As he retraced their conversation, I stole a quick look at Nancy. I'm sure we read each other's thoughts, for we identified so strongly with what was happening in the lives of these friends.

"I told Judy that I had invited the Lord into my life, and if she would just give me a chance, I'd show her that Jesus Christ could make a new man out of me."

Paul chuckled at himself as he described what happened next. "It's strange how the human mind works," he said. "I gathered all the liquor from the cabinets and set it by the sink. As I looked at it, my first thought was to call someone and give it away; that was a lot of money sitting there. Then I realized that would be a big mistake. As I picked up the last bottle, I thought maybe I ought to keep just one in case someone who drinks should come by to visit." He shook his head and said, "I realized then, that last bottle was the most important one of all to pour out . . . and I did it."

We laughed together as Paul went back over all those times that I had been such a pest to him.

"Remember that football banquet?" he asked. "That was the first time I ever saw you—and I could hardly wait to hear you. You were everything I expected a former professional football player to be: big, tough, and kinda' mean looking with that scar across your upper lip. You looked just like what I wanted to be when you got up to speak. Then, before you finished, you started talking about Jesus and what He had done for you. Man, I could have killed you! When I got to the car that night, I told Judy, 'I can't believe the school would allow that religious nut to come and spoil the whole thing. Having people pray—I can't believe it!' I was really fuming!"

I've been told I come on strong. I've always come on strong; God just channeled my intensity for His purposes. When the Lord tamed "The Bull," He replaced aggression with love, and contrary to popular belief, love is not a passive, docile emotion. Love is incredible, supernatural action. Love moves everything in its path. When Jesus called those simple fishermen to follow Him, He was not demoting them. He was giving them the highest commission. To be searchers for souls is a commandment, not a gift!

21

Unseen Links

In August 1977 newspaper headlines all over the world announced "The King Is Dead!" Elvis Presley, the king of rock and roll, had died at Graceland in Memphis. As I walked into my house on August 17, the day following his death, the phone was ringing. A man identifying himself as Bob Starr from a Miami radio station asked to speak to Bull Bramlett. "Speaking," I said.

"Are you the same Bull Bramlett who used to play football for the Miami Dolphins?"

"No, this is not the same Bull Bramlett. This is a different one. In 1973, I invited Jesus Christ to come into my heart and life, to become my Lord and my Savior. I repented of my sins, and I have never been the same."

He said, "I can see that this is a different Bull Bramlett." Then he told me, "We are live on radio, Bull. We know that you grew up with Elvis, and we want you to tell us what is going on in Memphis on the day after his death."

"I don't know a lot about what is happening other than the shock everyone is experiencing right now. But I do know that 'it is appointed unto men once to die, but after this the judgment.'¹ Since I've given my life to the Lord, I know this is the important issue that we all must face." Bob Starr listened while I shared my testimony on his live radio program.

The next day I received a similar call from a radio station in Los Angeles. This conversation was also heard on live radio. I was as proud of Elvis as anyone. Here was a poor boy who had bought himself a $12.95 guitar at age 13 and taught himself to play it. Without ever learning to read music, he surpassed and amazed successful, popular musicians of an entire era, appealing to people of all ages. What he achieved with his music was great, but when someone dies, it is an opportunity for all who are alive to realize that one day they, too, will draw their last breath here. A death is God's reminder to us to be ready to meet Him.

A few days after the phone call from Miami, a reporter from *The Boston Globe* came through Memphis on his way to Elvis' birthplace, Tupelo, Mississippi, to prepare a series of articles. As we talked I told the reporter that I had not seen Elvis for some time, but I hoped Elvis had met Jesus before it was too late. I would never have known how my comment was used had I not had a strange request from an elderly Jewish man in New York City.

The phone rang one night at eleven o'clock. A high, reedy voice on the other end said, "This is Abraham Segal. I am looking for the Bull Bramlett that used to play professional football." I told him that he had found the right man, and he began explaining how he had heard of me.

"I was walking down the street in New York City," Abraham said, "when I looked down and saw a newspaper at my feet. The headline read, 'Bull Bramlett Hopes Elvis Met Jesus Before It Was Too Late.' I read the entire article and decided to call you."

Mr. Segal had grown up in a huge apartment complex. While he was a young boy, a Jewish woman who lived there gave him a New Testament and told him, "If you want to meet your Messiah, read this aloud. Somewhere in these pages, as you read, you will meet your Messiah."

"That was many years ago," Mr. Segal continued. "I began to read that little New Testament. You know, Mr. Bramlett, 'faith cometh by hearing, and hearing by the word of God,'[2] and just like the woman promised, as I read aloud, I met my Messiah. The Lord Jesus came into my heart and changed my life."

Then Abraham Segal made what seemed to me a strange request. "The vacant lots and parks of New York City are full of young people who get together to play football and other games. With your background as a former professional athlete, you can help me reach these young people with the message of Christ. I want to use your testimony in witnessing to them. Could you send me some materials on your career and on your experience as a Christian?"

"I certainly will, sir," I told him.

I have often thought of the providence that used the death of Elvis Presley in Memphis, Tennessee, to call young people who lived twelve hundred miles away to Christ.

The evening I returned home from a speaking tour in Canada, feeling completely worn out, I was sound asleep when a phone call came from a Memphis hospital. John Biggs, father of my former Humes schoolmate Bobby Biggs, was on the line. He asked if I was the John Bramlett who had gone to Humes High School, and I told him I was. He told me he was suffering from emphysema, a blood clot in his leg, and a disc problem in his back. He then asked me to come to the hospital and tell him about Jesus.

"John, I have kept up with you all through school and college and have followed your pro football career. I know a lot more about you than you may realize. I know how mean you were before you changed, and if God could do that for you, I want Him to do that for me. Will you come?"

"Yes, sir, I surely will."

I went out to the hospital and we had a long talk. I told him how God had changed my heart, shared some of my experiences with Him, and read Scriptures to him about how to be saved. He prayed to receive Christ, and God set John Biggs free. As I read verses of assurance to him, he said, "You know, John, I've been a churchgoing man, but I knew that I was not right with God. My son, Bobby, a preacher has witnessed to me, and others have preached to me."

"Well, just be thankful that you finally came to the place of wanting Jesus in your life enough to believe in Him."

He told me he had heard Bobby use stories about me many times to illustrate the power of God to change people. "As I thought about you, John, I decided that if God could make a new man out of you, the way you were, then maybe He could do something for me."

While I was there, Bobby called his dad, and it was great to see the happiness in the older man's face as he told his son that they had the same Lord.

As we rejoiced over his new-found peace and joy, I said, "Mr. Biggs, I know how you feel. I wasted thirty-one years of my life."

He replied, "John, I have wasted seventy-four years, but I won't waste another minute. I'll be living for the Lord and telling people about Jesus from now on."

This man's son, a minister, and others, had witnessed to him. They had planted the seed. At long last, it had taken root in his heart. Every Christian is responsible for planting and for watering, but it is "God that giveth the increase."[3]

I learned a valuable lesson in that experience with John Biggs. There is something very reassuring about witnessing to a person who is ready to respond eagerly to what you have to say—but when it doesn't happen that way, what then? I couldn't stop thinking about those people who had repeatedly shared the gospel with John. I felt that God was showing me the larger picture of how He uses Christians working together in His own time and in His own way.

As I drove away after seeing John Biggs, I spoke aloud to the Savior, "Thank you, Lord Jesus, for working in my life, and for letting me have a part in seeing others come to know you."

In a few short weeks I'd seen so many lives turned around that my cup was running over. Only two weeks earlier in Houston I had met an old friend whom I had not seen since 1962, and we had rejoiced together in being Christian brothers. I had played football against Johnny Baker when he was an All-American at Mississippi State University. In the Blue-Gray game of '62, Johnny and I were co-captains for the South.

I was in Houston to speak at a Professional Athletes Outreach conference and to preach a revival in Pasadena, Texas. I called Johnny. He had already heard that I was a Christian, but like many others, he found it difficult to believe. As Johnny listened to me tell about my new life, he realized that John Bramlett really knew and loved the Lord. We laughed and cried together as we shared experiences of God's grace in our lives.

Before leaving Houston, Nancy and I visited with Johnny and his family in their home. While we were there, Johnny, who has been blessed materially as well as spiritually, gave me seven suits. I never have a surplus of clothes; I trust God for everything I need, and He has always provided. This time His provision was overwhelming—I had never owned seven suits at once!

Johnny's arms are longer than mine and he is taller, so the suits needed alterations. After I got home, I took them to a shop so they would be ready later that week, since I was going out of town for several speaking engagements. I was to leave on Wednesday, and had arranged to pick up the suits at four o'clock on Tuesday afternoon. When I went to get them, I was told to come back at six. I got busy with others things, so I sent Andy and Don to get the suits at six. They came back with the news that the suits would be finished at eight. I went to the shop at eight o'clock, and the suits were still unfinished.

By then, only one man remained in the shop working, so I sat down to wait. As I sat there while the young man finished my suits, I suddenly remembered the story of Philip and the Ethiopian eunuch, when the angel of the Lord sent Philip to the desert to win the eunuch to Jesus Christ.

I felt the Spirit of God urging me to witness to the young man, and he seemed eager to hear. Before I left, he made a personal commitment to the Lord. Already, before I had a chance to wear them, Johnny Baker's suits had helped win a soul to Christ. And I received a little lesson in patience as I understood why the suits were not ready at four o'clock—or six—or even eight; arrangements were being made for that young man to have an opportunity to meet Jesus.

"Lord, Jesus, help us to realize that every person who rejects You is in a prison of his own making." In 1979 I became involved in a vital, ongoing struggle for souls on one of the most complex battlegrounds of all—a prison crusade. I joined a group of Christian laymen in the Florida Prison Crusade led by Jim Williams, a dedicated member of First Baptist Church of Jacksonville, Florida, and a great soul winner.

The many businessmen who support this ministry are instrumental in the continuing work of bringing lost prison inmates to Christ. Some of these inmates will never again experience the freedom of going outside stone walls, but their spirits can be set free to live a changed life even in prison.

On that first crusade, I met Harold Morris. Harold spent almost ten years in Georgia State Penitentiary, falsely accused and convicted of armed robbery and murder. Like so many of the boys and girls of today, Harold had been running with the wrong kind of people, had a bad attitude, and foolishly involved himself in crime without any intention of becoming a criminal. When he was finally released in 1978 from the horrors of prison, he was able to expand the new life he had already begun with Jesus Christ while incarcerated. On the inside, his changed position had made him a respected witness to the love of Jesus for lost souls, and now that he was free, Harold was going back inside as often as he could to keep up that witness.

We became friends, and as Harold and I listened to each other, we discovered many similarities in our old attitudes. My own early rebellion caused almost all my problems in the first thirty-one years of my life.

Men in the crusade who witness to inmates face an entirely different kind of audience. No peaches and roses here. Hardened criminals are not concerned with sparing a man's feelings; some would rather spit on you than listen to you. They are quick to sense insincerity of purpose. I've learned that there are two groups of people who are not easily fooled: kids, who have a way of seeing through a fake concern, and prison inmates, who have seen it all. Those who witness inside prison walls have to love the men and women there enough to risk rejection in its strongest form—and go on loving!

The amazing ways God calls people are often unseen, but I think He sometimes allows us to see Him at work as a special reward. I find that the more I trust when I can't see, the more I'm allowed to see later on.

Mickey Parrish demonstrated to me how far a man will go who loves his fellow man. Already involved in prison crusade work, he had an opportunity to go into the prisons of Africa. He became so impressed with the need there for the message of freedom in Christ that upon returning home he felt compelled to take a drastic step of faith. Mickey sold his business and left his home in Jacksonville. He and his wife, Alice, moved to Africa to work there in a prison ministry called Christian Light Foundation.

In 1986 Mickey invited a team from the United States to minister inside African prisons, and I was included. Others on the team were Paul Wrenn, the 1981 Super Power heavyweight lifting champion of the world, and John Nill, a singer with a beautiful tenor voice.

Not quite sure what to expect, I prepared as well as I knew how to share my testimony. But not one of us on the team was prepared for the depressing misery in those African prisons. I spent the whole week crying over wasted lives and lost opportunities. I gave all the money I had with me to try to upgrade conditions for those I talked to; while sick at heart, I realized how unchanged their situation would be by tomorrow.

It was hard to leave while even one remained who may never have another chance to know Jesus. After a week of looking into empty eyes and hopeless faces, I understood the motivation that kept Mickey and Alice Parrish working in Africa.

"Thank You, Lord Jesus, for keeping me on my face before You, for even as I praise You for the 'ninety and nine' who hear, I cannot forget those who are lost without You. Thank You for Your amazing ways—that even the joy of Your blessing deepens the hunger for a greater commitment."

22

Full Circle

"My goal in life was to follow in my dad's footsteps and do the things he did. I wanted to be just like him. My brother Andy and I talked about how we were going out drinking and fighting with Dad; then when I was in the fifth grade, my dad threw us a curve. He became a Christian, and everything changed. No more angry fits at home, no more going out drinking—just love, and living for the Lord, going to church, and witnessing to others about what Jesus had done in his life."

I was sitting in the pulpit behind the speaker in a small church in Ripley, Mississippi. The congregation listened attentively as the young man shared a personal testimony of God's grace in his life. And suddenly, as I looked out across the crowded room, I saw another congregation in another Mississippi church. With a shock, I realized that on the same date, ten years earlier, this same young man had stood before a similar audience in a small church in Mississippi giving personal testimony of the saving grace of Jesus in his life.

I remembered that morning ten years before as if it were yesterday. I had accepted an invitation to speak at the little church, and at the last minute before leaving home, I said to my fourteen-year-old, who was a new Christian, "Don, why don't you go with me? You can share your testimony before I speak. Just tell the people how you got saved and how you love Jesus. You need to start doing that."

I've never tried to put words in either of my boys' mouths when they are going to speak for the Lord, because I figure He can do a much better job than I could. So I had no idea what fourteen-year-old Don was likely to tell in church that morning.

We arrived early and sat down on the front bench with our backs to the door. The pastor came, and as he talked with us, I realized that the church was filling up, but Don sat there without once looking behind him. Before I went to the pulpit to speak, the pastor announced that my son would share his testimony. I'd been sitting there admiring Don's composure. When he stood up and turned around, at his first glimpse of the packed house, he almost went into shock.

He jumped back like he'd been shot and said, "Daddy, look at all those people!"

I said, "That's all right, Son. They just came to hear about Jesus."

They heard about the Lord that morning in that little church in Mississippi. The first words out of old Don's mouth got their attention. He said, "You folks don't know my daddy. Some of you may think you know somebody that's mean—but folks, my daddy was *mean!*"

He talked for only five minutes, but Don talks fast, and when he sat down, I really couldn't see what I was doing there. The Spirit of Jesus came over the people that morning as they listened to a young boy tell what it meant to him to have a Christian home.

Many decisions were made at the close of the service, decisions that must have altered some homes. I wanted to encourage Don to witness without planting any seeds of pride, so on the way home I said, "Hey, Son, wasn't it great to see the way people responded?"

"Yeah, they really do love Jesus. But Dad, you didn't mind what I said about you being mean before you met Jesus, did you?"

"Son, you did just right. If you didn't tell 'em how bad I was before, they couldn't see what a difference it makes to know the Lord."

As I sat there in Ripley thinking of the past, Don's mention of football brought me back to the present: " . . . and taking me down with that knee injury requiring surgery was the best thing God could have done for me at that time. He had to put me on my back so I'd look up and see Him. Through that time when I was unable to play, God showed me that I couldn't look to football for happiness, I couldn't look to Mom and Dad for happiness. The only happiness that lasts is in Jesus Christ, and the reason it lasts is because no matter how bad things get, Jesus is still in your heart, there with you through it all."

I could see that Don was coming to a close. "I love football as much as ever. When we won the 1986 National Championship at Carson-Newman College and I was selected as the Most Valuable Player of the championship game, I was grateful for the opportunity being interviewed by the news media gave me. It meant so much to be able to say to the television audience and to the press, 'Yes, this is wonderful, but the greatest thing that ever happened to me was when I became a Christian.'"

"And I think it is important for you to know that from the day my dad became a Christian, he taught my brother and me that following the Lord is the most important thing; it's not sports, or money, or pleasure, but knowing God. I wish every kid could have the kind of home my dad and my mother have given Andy and me. In closing, I want to share with you 2 Corinthians 5:17, a favorite to us because it has come true in the lives of our whole family: 'Therefore if any man be in Christ, he is a new creature: old things are passed away; behold all things are become new.'"

Don sat down. After I mopped my eyes and thought I could trust my voice, I told the people I considered my sons a hard act to follow. "It's like this," I explained, "as grateful as I am to God for changing me, and as full of joy as I am to have Jesus in my heart, my two sons and my wife knew me before I met Jesus. They knew the dark side of me better than anyone else, including me. I couldn't see it the way it really was because about half the time I was drunk, and when I wasn't drunk I was trying to justify what I did while I was drunk. My family lived through hell on earth until God did what seemed impossible. I'm living proof that the things which are impossible to man are not only possible to God but absolutely certain when His conditions are met. After my wife, Nancy, was saved and began praying for me, and after she recruited her Christian friends to start praying for me, those 'impossible' things began to happen!"

As I began preaching from John's gospel, Jesus had never been more real, more alive, or more exciting to me. "Jesus didn't call us to be dead, dull, dormant Christians—and I am never surprised when people respond to the preaching of God's Word. I know they are not coming in answer to my appeal, nor in fear of my judgment. All I ask is to be allowed to stand behind the cross and give lost people a clear view of it."

I have no trouble finding those who crave the abundant life; the problem arises when they are told that life comes by the cross. I agree, there is no joy in death itself, whether it's on a cross or on a sickbed. But there can be no abundance of life, no life eternal, until that old sinful heart is crucified with Christ by faith in what He did. I just try to help people see that after the cross had served its purpose, Jesus was resurrected to life.

He hung on the cross only long enough to do what He came to do. When I accepted the death sentence of my sins, I became crucified with Christ—then, in the sweet name of Jesus, I could share in His newness of life. There is no way to cheat death; we are all going to meet it one way or another.

> And he said to them all, If any man will come after me, let him deny himself, and take up his cross daily, and follow me. For whosoever will save his life shall lose it: but whosoever will lose his life for my sake, the same shall save it.[1]

God wants us involved in healing hurting people, but that can't happen unless we care enough to offer ourselves in a spirit of love. When I met Curt Taylor at a weight-lifting room near where I played racquetball, I had no idea how much he was hurting and in need of God's healing power. I started stopping by to talk to him about Jesus, but he didn't seem interested. I learned that he was divorced, so I shared some of the details of how Nancy and I had found a new closeness in Christ. He told me then that his former wife, Gracie, lived in Washington, D.C., and had been out of his life for two years.

Curt went to Tupelo, Mississippi, on business, and Jake Mills invited him to a Bible study in his home. I had met Jake when several years previously, I had spoken in a Presbyterian church in Tupelo. He'd come to church that evening out of curiosity because of all the bad stories he had heard about my early life. But after I spoke, Jake came down to the altar and fell to his knees. When he got up he was on fire for the Lord, and that fire is still burning. I am sure it was no accident that in addition to his distributorship with Shell Oil Company, he had also gone to work for Curt's business, Taylor Machinery Company.

In the home of Jake and Jane Mills that night in Tupelo, Curt committed his life to Christ. After returning home, he called Gracie and asked if he could visit her. She invited him to Washington and immediately afterward, the Lord gave them a nudge in the right direction by arranging a job transfer for Gracie to Nashville, Tennessee.

It was only a matter of months before Curt led Gracie to the Lord—and to the marriage altar. When he asked me to be his best man at the wedding, I said, "Man, that's an honor I wouldn't want to miss!"

It felt great to hear them repeat the vows that this time they entrusted to the One who brought them back together. Because of God's power to heal broken lives, two beautiful little girls, Tish and Sally Taylor, are growing up in a unified Christian home.

Looking back at the unrestrained defiance of my life in the years before I trusted Jesus, I'm thankful to have returned to many of the scenes of my rebellion and to have encountered many of the victims of my insensitive acts. In Denver I have preached in churches near some of the "joints" I used to hang out in. What a privilege to demonstrate to people that God still has the power to change a life; all they had ever seen or heard of me was that I was a troublemaker and a drunk.

The St. Louis Cardinals and the Kansas City Chiefs played an exhibition game in Memphis, giving me the opportunity to witness to players from both teams. I gave my testimony in the Cardinals' chapel service at their hotel, in which several players made decisions to live for Christ. In every meeting place, I find good people who don't murder, don't commit adultery, don't drink or steal, and may even go to church—but they are lost without God.

In Tulsa at Steve Largent's invitation to speak at the Fellowship of Christian Athlete's banquet, I was touched by the sweet Spirit of Jesus in the home of this fine professional athlete and his wife, Terry. While I was there, I learned that Howard Twilley, one of my former teammates in Miami, lived in Tulsa. Howard was a Christian even then, and remembering my behavior toward him in those days sent a surge of shame through my heart.

I talked with Howard before leaving Tulsa, and as I apologized to this fine former wide receiver, he stopped me to say, "Bull, we are brothers in Christ. We don't need to be looking back; we love each other! Man, I'm just happy that we *both* know Jesus."

In Macon, Georgia, for a speaking engagement, I remembered that this was the home of the former baseball pitcher I had swung outside the window of a Duluth, Minnesota, hotel, eleven stories above the street. I looked up Charlie Haygood's telephone number. I had not spoken to Charlie for twenty-one years. When he answered the phone, I asked, "Charlie Haygood, who was the meanest man you ever met?"

Without a moment's hesitation, he answered, "John Bramlett—and no one else is even close."

"Charlie, this is 'Bull.' I'm in Macon, and I want to see you. I need to talk to you."

He and his wife, Ellen, met me for dinner that evening. After a wonderful time of sharing many experiences of God's grace in the years since we had seen each other, Charlie said, "No one could ever have convinced me that you could be turned around, John. You were too far gone. If everyone who knew you then could see you now, they wouldn't doubt the power of God." In parting, Charlie added, "Man, this is the 'Bull' I'm going to remember. God has helped me through some tough times, but He worked a miracle with you!"

I've found joy in coming full circle for another chance with people I have failed in the past.

I am not a licensed evangelist—I am not an ordained minister. I am a layman, saved by the grace of God, and called out as a witness to the sweetness of walking with Jesus. When He saved me, He gave me a love in my heart for all those who are as lost today as I was before I met Him.

Letters and calls of encouragement from brothers and sisters in Christ remind me daily of the only source of a power to change lives. This, from Chuck Slabaugh, keeps prayer alive in my heart for all the young men and young women who started out with the world by the tail and ended up in the gutter.

Dear John,

Thanks, John, for taking the time to call me last November, and sending me that little New Testament. I've searched the pages of that little guide and found truth, purpose, meaning & direction. Nothing can compare to the power of Christ in changing a life! I will pray for your ministry because I know you are a tremendous threat to Satan, and he will attack you in any way possible. If you ever feel somewhat ineffective, just think of me & how God used you to bring an outcast, bitter, drug addict into the Kingdom of God. I remember my family wouldn't even let me stay with them last February, '86, because they were afraid I would go berserk and kill them. I stayed with my grandmother, who later told me, if I killed her, it would be better than killing someone else because she was old. 5 Drug Rehabilitation Centers & 2 State Hospitals & I was still hopelessly lost. Only the power of Christ can truly set a person free. Psalm 34 has become one of my favorite scriptures. I know it means as much to you as it does to me. It tells of Gods powerful, protective plan for those who put their trust in him. Isn't that great? I love you, my brother, and thanks again.

Your brother in Christ,
Chuck.

P.S. Could you send a few more New Testaments to me, to share with others God's Plan of Salvation? Thanks!

I wish every young person reading these words could personally realize the power and mercy of Almighty God.

As for "Bull" Bramlett, who always wanted to play for a winner, he finally realized his dream. The preeminent coach paid the supreme penalty to get "Bull," and He gave him a no-cut contract for all eternity.

Thank you, Lord Jesus!

At last, I'm on the winning team.

Notes

9. Just Call Me "Bull"

   1. Galatians 6:7
   2. Proverbs 13:15
   3. Proverbs 14:12

16. Another Chance

   1. Matthew 5:38–39
   2. Matthew 5:46
   3. 1 John 5:1
   4. 1 Corinthians 15:1–2
   5. 1 Corinthians 6:9–10
   6. 2 Corinthians 5:21
   7. John 3:16

17. "You're Not Bull Bramlett!"

   1. Matthew 6:33
   2. John 10:10
   3. Psalm 126:5
   4. Psalm 126:6

18. Turning the Corner

   1. 1 Corinthians 9:24–25

19. "All I Want for Christmas"

   1. Psalm 116:15
   2. Proverbs 22:15
   3. Romans 10:17

20. The Power in a Tamed Bull

   1. Ephesians 4:32

21. Unseen Links

   1. Hebrews 9:27
   2. Romans 10:17
   3. 1 Corinthians 3:7

22. Full Circle

   1. Luke 9:23–24

About the Authors

John "Bull" Bramlett continues to share his powerful, personal testimony and Christian message at churches, high schools, colleges, and prisons. He is also a widely sought speaker for civic and business groups, and for the Fellowship of Christian Athletes.

If you would like him to speak to your group, he can be reached at:

John Bramlett Ministries
P.O. Box 1747
Cordova, Tennessee 38088

Tula Jeffries is a gifted writer that wrote a weekly inspirational column for *The Daily News* of Richmond, Missouri for many years. She is the author of *"Singleness of Purpose"* and *"Taming the Bull"*. She now makes her home in Nashville, Arkansas and is active in her church there.